wool toys
& friends

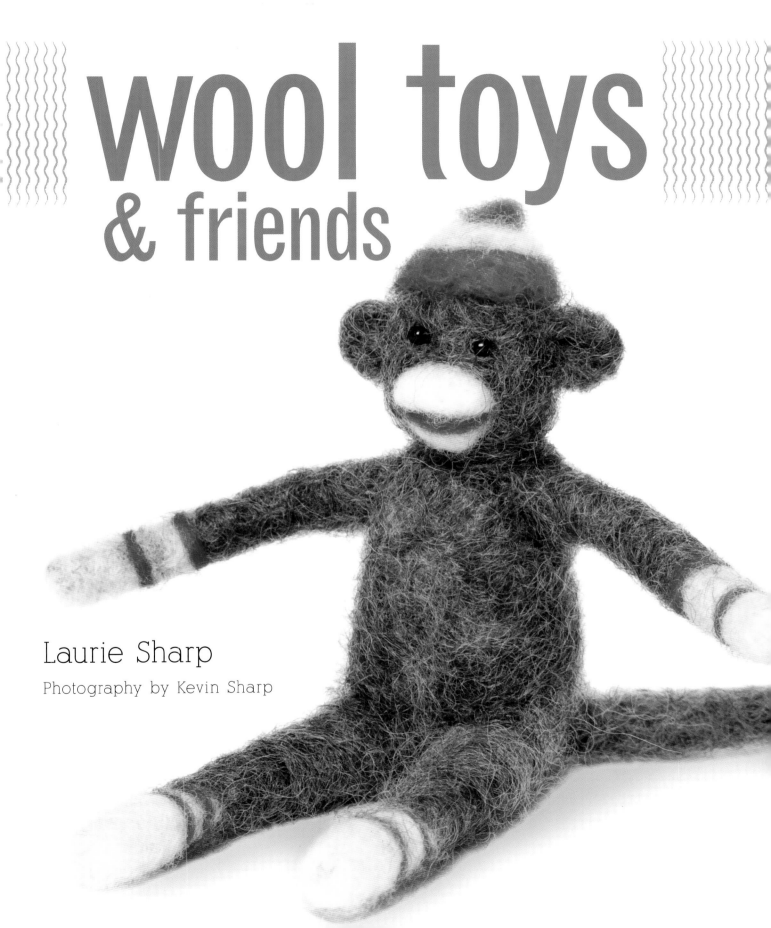

Laurie Sharp

Photography by Kevin Sharp

First published in the United States of America by
Creative Publishing international, Inc., a member of
Quayside Publishing Group
400 First Avenue North
Suite 300
Minneapolis, MN 55401
1-800-328-3895
www.creativepub.com

Library of Congress Cataloging-in-Publication Data

Sharp, Laurie.
  Wool toys and friends : step-by-step instructions for needle-felting
fun / Laurie Sharp ; photography by Kevin Sharp.
      p. cm.
  Summary: "Includes instructions for needle felting and wet felting of
wool fibers to shape them into toys and small figures suitable for
display. Step-by-step instructions with photographs"--Provided by
publisher.
  ISBN-13: 978-1-58923-506-9 (hard cover)
  ISBN-10: 1-58923-506-1 (hard cover)
  1. Felt work. 2. Felting. 3. Toy making. I. Title.

  TT849.5.S532 2010
  746'.0463--dc22

  2009043200

Photography: Kevin Sharp
Copy Editor: Catherine Broberg
Proofreader: Karen Ruth
Book Design: Judy Morgan
Page Layout: Wendy Lutge
Cover Design: everlution design

Printed in China
10 9 8 7 6 5 4 3

contents

introduction

Playthings inspire imagination and release our inhibitions. The whimsical nature of handcrafted toys and small figures can invite humor and joy.

Toys and playthings are not just for children. High-quality, heirloom toys are collected and admired by young and old alike. Those fortunate enough to receive a handmade toy as a gift often treasure them as works of art.

Yet the artworks made through using this book are also toys that are meant to be played with. Though their small parts, such as beads and wheels, make them unsuitable for children under age three, older children—and even adults—will delight in the feel and character of these toys. Parents, grandparents, and older siblings can set an example of how to gently handle these special, handmade toys. Perhaps they'll be saved for special occasions, such as long car rides or airplane trips. Or maybe they'll earn the spot on someone's bed and become a nighttime

snuggly companion. Some of the toys, such as the felted pumpkin house and mouse, may actually become stronger with play because the moist, warm child's hands cause the wool to felt just a bit more.

The joy of these projects is not limited to their final form. Indeed, toy making in itself is a fun and creative endeavor. The process of making these toys combines sculpting, painting, sewing, and woodworking, allowing you to "play" in a number of ways. The shaping and sculpting techniques with wet and needle felting can be extended to create interesting and sophisticated sculptures. All of the techniques used are easy to learn, and the materials are simple and readily available.

Don't be afraid to take on these projects, even if you have limited or no experience working with wool or wool felt. A little preparation is all that's required. Before you get started, read through the information about materials and techniques. If you have never wet felted or needle felted before, practice a little before you get going with your first project. You may even decide to invite youngsters to help with these creations. Most children age nine and up have enough dexterity to use the felting needle. Just be sure to have them work with an adult in the beginning, as the needle is very sharp. Giving them the opportunity to be creative is a gift in itself. Older children often find toy making to be very satisfying.

The last and most important tip before you dive into these projects is to have fun! I think you will soon discover why I am so passionate about this craft.

Most of the projects in this book require simple materials.
Resources for where to find these items are listed on page 121.

materials

Wool

When the sheep is sheared, the nicest parts of the fleece are picked free of debris, washed, and put through a large carding machine. The result is wool batting—fluffy layers of wool fibers scattered in different directions.

The next step is to align the fibers so that they are facing the same direction and form a smooth rope or roving. Most of the wool you will use for projects in this book is available in roving form.

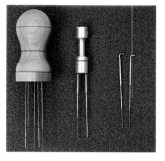

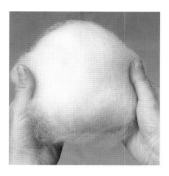

Roving needs to be prepared before you begin using it for felting. You will need to mess up the aligned fibers so that they are more perpendicular to each other. Do this by pulling an 18" (45.7 cm) long piece of roving into several long, thin strips. Pull these strips in half and layer again. Repeat until the wool roving seems fluffier.

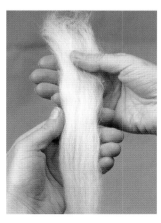

Wool Felt Fabric

When wool is felted into flat sheets either by hand or by machine, it is called wool felt or simply, felt fabric. Some wool felt fabric is a combination of wool and rayon or nylon. If you compare generic synthetic felt to wool felt, you will easily see the difference in quality between the types. If you are going to spend the time making something by hand, high-quality wool felt is well worth the cost.

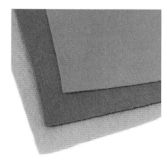

Woven Wool Flannel

Wool flannel is made differently than felt. Flannel is a woven material made with wool thread rather than cotton or polyester. It is not as heavy as some felt fabric. Wool flannel is a good surface for the application of needle felting because of its woven texture, which allows the felting needle to penetrate more smoothly and easily compared to felt fabric.

Materials for Needle Felting

Only a few materials are necessary for needle felting: a felting needle, foam, and wool. A needle punch or other object that can hold more than one needle at a time is good to have on hand for some of the projects that require felting over a large area.

Materials for Wet Felting

Wet felting uses hot, soapy water to felt the wool. Some of the projects in the book are made using this method and again, only a few easy-to-find materials are required:

- warm water—2 cups is generally enough
- spray bottle
- towel
- dish soap
- 2 mm thick foam template, cut according to the pattern
- bubble wrap—10" (25.4 cm) square piece
- plastic bag—small
- wool—refer to individual projects for amount needed

You will need a few tools and other items to complete some of projects in this book. Here's a list of things to have on hand before you begin.

tools and extras

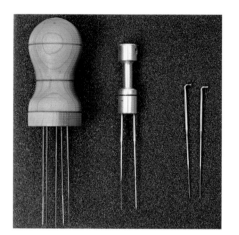

Felting needles and various needle holders are some of the most important tools you will need. The needles are available at craft stores and the holders can be found in a variety of types and sizes. Experiment with holders to see which ones are most comfortable in your hand.

A 38-gauge triangle needle is the size used for all of the projects in this book.

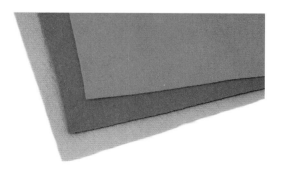

Wool felt from Holland is the best quality for wool playthings. This type of felt is available online and in specialty fabric stores. If you cannot find 100% wool felt, a felt blend with rayon works well.

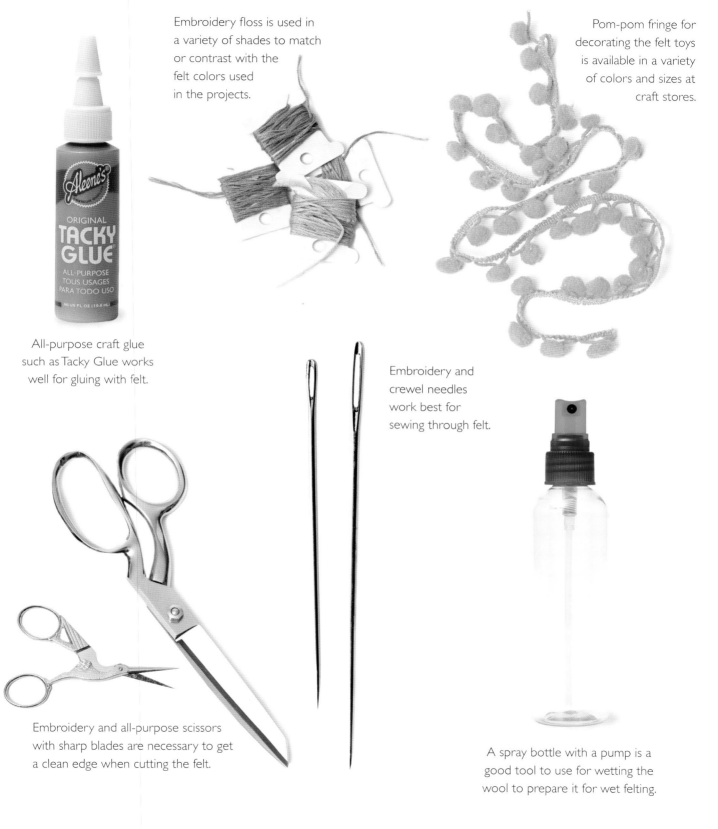

Embroidery floss is used in a variety of shades to match or contrast with the felt colors used in the projects.

Pom-pom fringe for decorating the felt toys is available in a variety of colors and sizes at craft stores.

All-purpose craft glue such as Tacky Glue works well for gluing with felt.

Embroidery and crewel needles work best for sewing through felt.

Embroidery and all-purpose scissors with sharp blades are necessary to get a clean edge when cutting the felt.

A spray bottle with a pump is a good tool to use for wetting the wool to prepare it for wet felting.

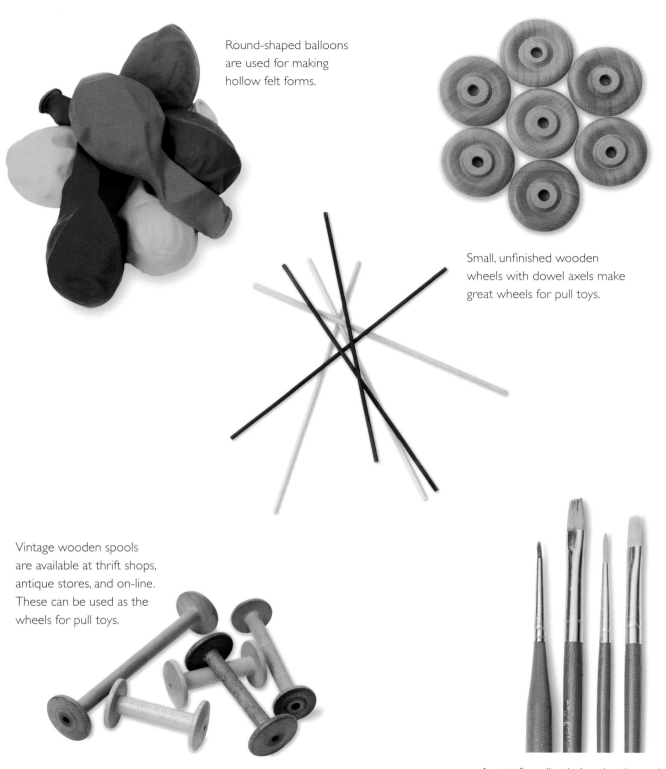

Round-shaped balloons are used for making hollow felt forms.

Small, unfinished wooden wheels with dowel axels make great wheels for pull toys.

Vintage wooden spools are available at thrift shops, antique stores, and on-line. These can be used as the wheels for pull toys.

A set of small paintbrushes is used to paint the wooden parts of the toys.

A pair of needle-nose pliers works well for shaping and cutting chenille stems.

Small black seed beads are used as eyes for the needle-felted animals.

A compass and pencil are very helpful for marking accurate circles and arc shapes.

Use black sewing thread—polyester or cotton/polyester blend—for sewing eyes on the animals.

Corsage pins are available at craft stores. To make custom sewing pins, cut off the pearl end with a heavy-duty wire cutter and replace it with a decorative bead. Epoxy glue works well for gluing on the bead.

Chenille stems are readily available and easy to cover with wool roving.

Two methods of felting are used to make wool toys and friends: needle felting and wet felting. Used in combination, these techniques allow for unlimited creativity with wool and wool felt.

basic techniques

Needle Felting

Needle felting uses a sharp, barbed needle to sculpt wool until it is felted into shape. Needle felting is a good technique to use if you are trying to make something small and detailed. You have more control over the amount of felting, how much wool you use, and how much area it will cover in comparison to wet felting. The difference is mainly in the amount of control you have in the wool as it goes from loose wool to felt.

The figures, dolls, and animals in this book are all needle felted. The instructions are slightly different, but all are put together in a similar way. Usually, a body form is made first.

Note: Throughout the book the words "needle" and "needling" are used as verbs to mean the act of needle felting, or repeatedly jabbing the wool using the felting needle.

Body

Measure the amount of wool required for the project. More wool is used in making the Elephant's body (page 82) as compared to the Prairie Dog (page 18). The measurements given in the instructions can be adjusted to suit the desired size of the finished piece. Tightly roll the wool into a barrel shape. Use your thumbs to fold the sides in as you roll so that the body is not too long and thin (A). Needle the surface of the wool all around to keep the fibers from unrolling and to help smooth the surface (B).

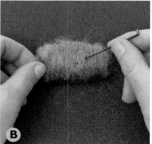

Head

Making the head is usually the next step in the needle-felting projects. To make a round head, measure the wool for that particular project and tightly roll it in a ball. Roll the strip of wool halfway up; then turn the ball and roll the rest of the strip around the top and bottom of the first roll. Needle to shape and hold the fibers in place (A).

To make a cone-shaped head, measure the wool for that particular project and roll into a cone shape. One end, the snout or nose end, should be narrower than the opposite end. Needle to shape and smooth the surface (B).

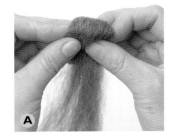

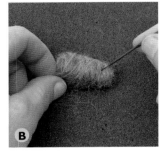

Appendages

Needle-felted animals and figures have different sized arms and legs, but the basic technique is the same for each. The arms and legs need to be very firm so that the figure is sturdy, especially if a child is going to play with it. The only exception is the pixie, which uses a chenille stem armature.

For each arm/leg, measure out the wool given in the instructions. Roll the strip of wool by twisting a wooden skewer and holding the wool tight as it wraps. One end should be narrow (hoof or hand) and the other end wider (thigh or shoulder) (A). Keep the fibers loose at the thigh or shoulder end to help with attachment. Needle all around the surface to help smooth the shape and keep it wrapped tight. Needle into the hoof or foot end to make it flat (B).

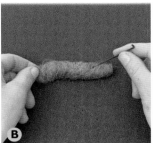

Wet Felting

Wet felting is the method familiar to most people. It involves using hot, soapy water and agitation to felt the wool. The scales on the wool fiber swell and expand when the wool is wet and as the wool is agitated, either by hand or machine. The scales become entangled and shrink together, thus forming felt.

There are many different methods of wet felting, but only simple techniques are required to make the projects in this book. With the instructions that follow, wet felting is done around a template which is removed to form a hollow shell or pocket.

Set up an area that is easy to clean up and near a sink. A kitchen table is good. Cover the surface with a towel. Lay the bubble wrap bumpy side up on the towel. The bumpy bubble wrap can help with the felting process, and the pockets between the bubbles helps hold some water to be absorbed as the wool is felted.

Cut a template in the desired shape from 2 mm craft foam. Begin the process by dividing the roving into several long, thin, wispy pieces. Lay the pieces of wool in crisscross layers over the template (A). This will help the scales on the wool tangle together. Keep in mind that the wool will shrink down to about half the size of the template by the time the process is complete.

Fill the spray bottle with warm water and a few teaspoons of dish soap; a small amount of soap is necessary to begin the felting process because soap allows some of the water to be absorbed by the wool and makes it easier to rub the surface of the wool without causing much disturbance to the layered fibers. Spray the surface of the wool pile (B).

Fold the wet fibers around the edge to the underside. Flip the template over and layer more wispy pieces of roving on the other side (C). The wool fibers should extend over the edge of the template slightly.

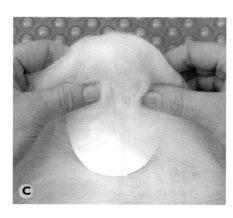

Lightly mold the layers to conform to the shape of the template (D).

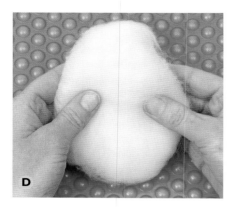

Spray the flip side with soapy water also. After the wool is wet, but not soaking, begin to massage from the center of the design out toward the edge. Add more water to areas that seem dry. It is tempting to rush, but massage for at least 5 minutes (E).

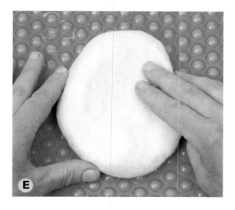

Optionally, if you find this too abrasive for your fingers, you can insert the wet, fiber-covered template into a small plastic bag and mas-sage from outside the bag.

Now do the pinch test: pinch some fiber on the surface of the wool. Ideally, the fibers should be sticking together and not come loose when pinched. If the fibers are loose and even become separated when pinched, keep massaging gently until the wool is firm. Once the wool gets past this point, cut a slit in the felt, and pull out the template (F), leaving a soggy fiber shell.

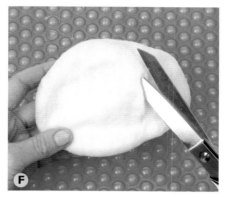

Now, begin the process of hardening the wool. There are many ways to harden the wool: rubbing it on a bumpy surface such as a washboard or bubble wrap or rolling it around in your hands will work (G). Work on both the inside and outside of the shell. Work with the wool for about 15 minutes or more.

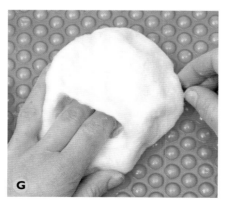

The wool can be stretched into shape at this point. If it seems dry, wet it before stretching it. The pumpkin (page 94) needs to be stretched into shape before drying.

Allow the wool to dry completely before needle felting so the needles won't rust. If desired, the hole can be sewn closed after the felt is dry.

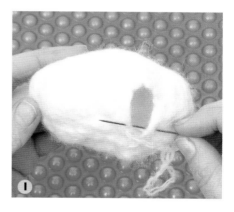

Embroidery

Wool felt fabric lends itself quite well to embroidery since it is sturdy and firm. Embroidery hoops are not necessary when using felt. There are only a few basic stitches needed for the felt book, felt house, and pop-up puppet projects.

Running Stitch

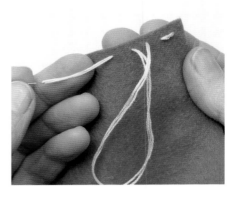

This stitch is used for sewing layers of wool felt together. Pile the layers of wool to be sewn together and stab through all the layers. Bring the needle up from the back, about ½" (1.3 cm) from where it first entered the fabric. Space the stitches evenly and keep their length even. Continue in a straight line. Tie a knot and cut at the end.

Blanket Stitch

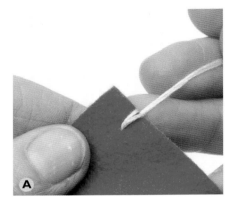

The blanket stitch is used for decorative edging on wool felt. First, thread an embroidery needle with two strands of embroidery floss; tie a knot at the end. Bring the needle and thread from the back, around the edge of the felt and back through, making a loop (A).

Bring the needle up through the edge of the felt, in the middle of the loop. Now put the needle in the felt about ¼" (6 mm) from the first stitch; pull the thread but not all the way through. Insert the needle through the loop and pull snug (B). This is the first stitch.

Continue to make a row of blanket stitches (C). Tie a knot and cut at the end.

French Knot

Bring the needle up from the back of the felt, wrap the floss once around the tip of the needle, and enter back into the felt (A), leaving a little knot on the surface (B).

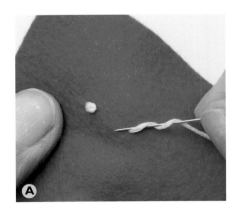

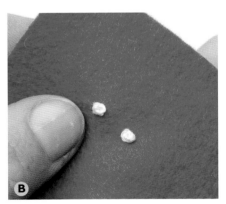

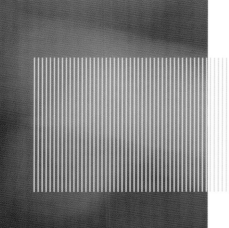

pop-up prairie dog puppet

The Prairie Dog Pop-Up is a delightful toy. With a simple twist of the dowel, the puppet can peek over the edge of the cone, slip back down, and then pop in surprise! Many other animals "pop up" from the ground—rabbits, moles, and badgers to name a few. The simple design of the puppet allows for creativity with embellishment on the felt cone. You can add beads, buttons, fringe or even decorative ribbons.

MATERIALS

- 0.2 oz. (6 g) light brown wool roving
- small amount of black wool
- 6" (15.2 cm) square piece of wool felt fabric
- 6" (15.2 cm) square piece of silk dupioni
- pattern (page 00)
- needle and thread
- black beads for eyes
- felting needle
- darning needle

- foam pad
- ruler
- 12" (30.5 cm) square piece of cardstock
- 12" (30.5) wooden dowel, 4 mm
- ribbon to decorate the cone
- glue
- scissors
- white acrylic paint and paintbrush
- pencil sharpener
- tape

CONE

1. Trace the pattern on a piece of cardstock and cut. Trace the same pattern on a piece of felt and cut. Trace the larger cone pattern on the silk and cut. Glue one edge of the silk cone to the card cone. Let dry.

2. Gently pull the pointed end of the silk upwards.

3. Ease the card into a cone shape.

4. Fold the card cone in half and tape to secure.

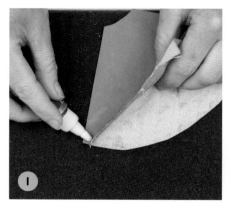

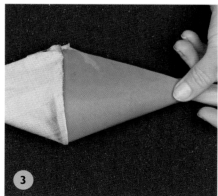
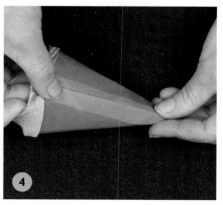

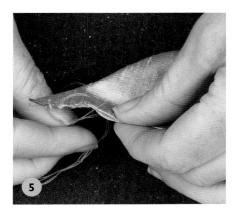

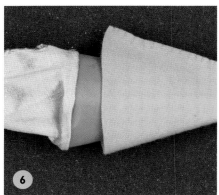

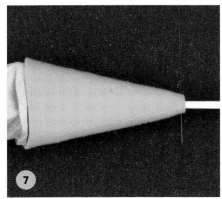

5. Stitch the sides of the silk cone together and stitch the sides of the felt cone together.

6. Slide the felt cone over the card and glue.

7. Use a pencil sharpener and sharpen both ends of the dowel to a point; then paint the dowel with white acrylic paint. Put a dot of glue on one of the pointed ends of the dowel and push through to the top of the silk cone. Let the glue dry.

(continued)

PRAIRIE DOG

8. Roll a 5" × 3" (12.7 × 7.6 cm) piece of light brown wool into a 2" (5.1 cm) long cone shape.

9. Roll a 3" × 2" (7.6 × 5.1 cm) piece of light brown wool into a 1" (2.5 cm) long cone shape.

10. Position the head on top of the body and needle to attach.

11. Needle two wisps of light brown wool into 1" (2.5 cm) round circles for the prairie dog's thighs.

12. Position the thighs on the side of the prairie dog's body and needle to attach.

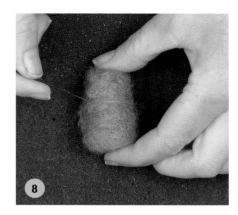

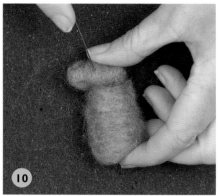

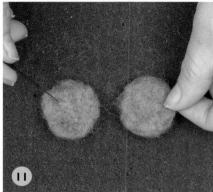

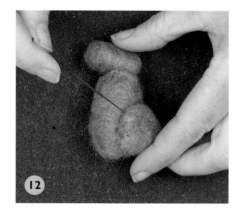

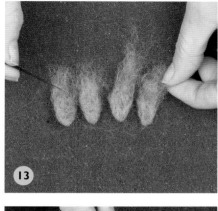

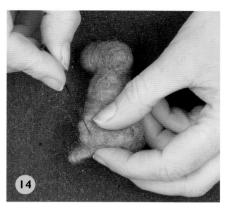

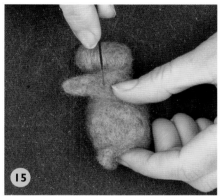

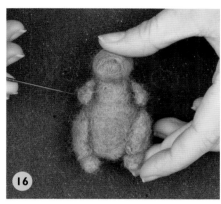

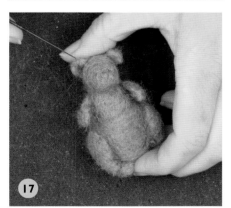

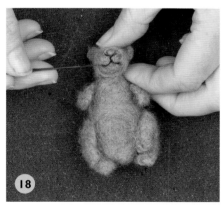

13. Fold a 1" (2.5 cm) long wisp of wool in half and needle to make a paw. Make four paws that measure ½" (1.3 cm).

14. Needle a paw to the bottom of the thigh on both sides of the prairie dog.

15. Position the other two paws on either side of the body and needle to attach.

16. Make sure the paws are even.

17. Needle two small wisps into tiny ears and attach to the prairie dog's head.

18. Needle a strip of black wool into a Y shape on the snout and needle a strip of black wool underneath the snout to make a mouth.

(continued)

19. Sew black beads on each side of the prairie dog's head for eyes.

20. Roll and needle a small piece of black wool on the back of the prairie dog for a tail.

21. Use the darning needle to make a hole in the bottom of the prairie dog. This is for inserting the silk-covered dowel.

22. Place a dot of glue on the end of the silk cone and twist the prairie dog onto the dowel.

23. Needle a piece of purple wool into a 1" (2.5 cm) round ball.

24. Put a dot of glue on the end of the dowel and twist the purple ball onto the dowel. Allow the glue to dry.

25. Decorate the cone with ribbon or trim, if desired.

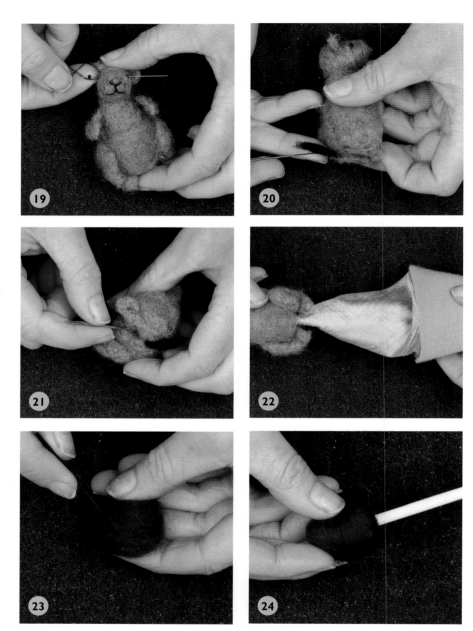

pixie

This little poseable pixie is quite the charmer, especially when sitting on top of a woolly toadstool. Wrapping and needling wool around a chenille stem armature allows the figure to be bent into all sorts of fun and comical poses.

MATERIALS

- two 12" (30.5 cm) white chenille stems
- 0.1 oz. (3 g) flesh-colored wool
- 0.3 oz. (9 g) green wool
- 5" x 2" (12.7 x 5.1 cm) piece of flesh-colored wool felt fabric
- small amount of brown and red wool

- darning needle
- needle-nose pliers
- felting needle
- foam pad
- glue
- ruler

ARMATURE

1. Bend one of the chenille stems in half and use the pliers to cut in half. One of the 6" (15.2 cm) pieces will be used for the arms. Bend the other stem in half. This will be the pixie's body, legs, and feet. Place the arm piece 1" (2.5 cm) below the top of the larger piece. Fold the larger piece over and around the arm piece, going through the legs. Make sure the arms and legs measure evenly. Set the body frame aside.

2. Roll a 5" x 2" (12.7 x 5.1 cm) piece of flesh-colored wool into a ball and needle to hold the fibers in place. Needle the ball until it measures 1½" (3.8 cm) wide. The face will be completed later.

   Rolling the ball of wool in your palms will help make it smooth.

3. Use a large sewing needle (darning needle) or awl to make a hole in the center of the ball to use for inserting the chenille stem.

4. Place a dab of glue on the head end of the chenille stem and twist it into the hole on the head.

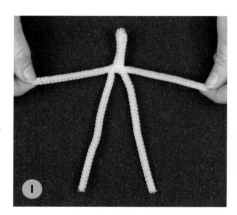
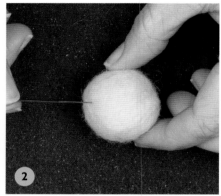
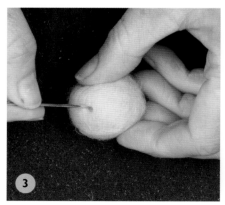
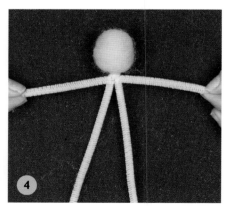

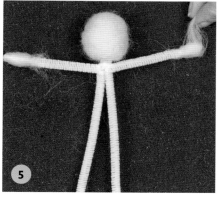

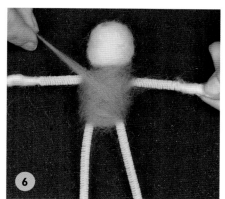

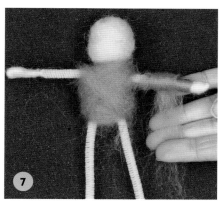

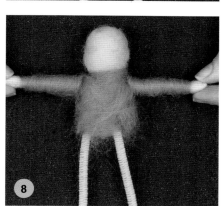

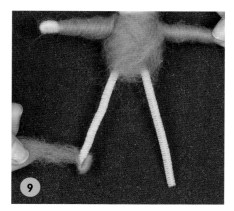

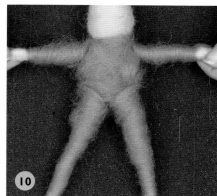

5. Wrap a wisp of flesh-colored wool around the hand end of the chenille stem and bend ½" (1.3 cm) in from the edge so that the sharp end of the chenille stem is folded in. Wrap another wisp of flesh-colored wool around the chenille stem to make a hand.

6. Begin to wrap the body. Take a small amount of green wool and wrap around the middle of the body. Crisscross layers of wool going from the shoulders across the body, under the other arm and back.

7. Wrap a 1" (2.5 cm) wisp of green wool around the arm starting at the wrist. Wrap evenly all the way up to the shoulder using many wispy layers of wool.

8. Repeat with the other arm.

9. Wrap the bottom inch (2.5 cm) of the chenille stem on each of the feet. Bend the pipe cleaner ½" (1.3 cm) from the bottom and wrap over the bend.

10. Continue to wrap the rest of the legs with wool. Once you are finished wrapping the body, check to see if any parts need wool so that it looks even. Needle all over the body to keep the wool in place. Take care not to stab into the pipe cleaner wire.

Try to wrap firmly and evenly. Avoid loose wrapping.

(continued)

11. Needle a 2" (5.1 cm) piece of green wool into a flat triangle shape. This will be the pixie's hat.

12. Fold the hat in half and needle up the side to close the seam. Place the hat on top of the pixie's head and needle all around the hat into the head to attach.

13. Needle a few wisps of brown wool into the pixie's forehead, right under the hat.

14. Needle a small ball of flesh-colored wool on the middle of the pixie's face for a nose.

15. Needle two wisps of brown wool on the face for eyes.

16. Needle some red wool on the face for a mouth.

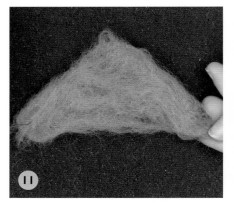

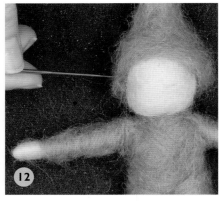

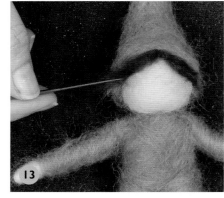

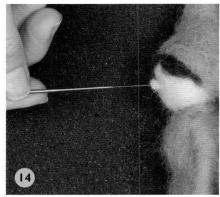

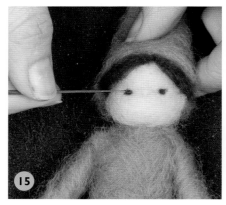

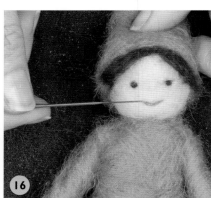

hedgehog
pincushion

The hedgehog pincushion is a great project for beginners. Her body, head, and legs are basic shapes and her curly wool locks disguise any slight "figure problems." The lanolin in Hedgie's wool is great for keeping all your pins and needles shiny and smooth.

MATERIALS

- 0.2 oz. (5 g) grey wool roving
- 0.25 oz. (7 g) camel-colored wool roving
- 0.25 oz. (7 g) grey curly wool locks
- small amount of black wool
- black beads for eyes

- darning needle
- wooden skewer
- felting needle
- foam pad
- ruler

HEDGEHOG BASE

1. Measure a 12" × 5" (30.5 × 12.7 cm) piece of gray wool for the hedgehog's body. Split the wool into several short strips and pile them one on top of the other. Needle felt the pile all over the surface and begin to form an oval shape by gently lifting the sides and needling them toward the center to create a rounded edge. The finished piece should measure 3½" (8.9 cm) long and 2½" (6.4 cm) wide. Set this piece aside.

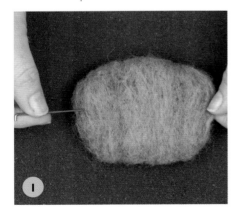

HEDGEHOG HEAD

2. Measure a 2" × 6" (5.1 × 15.2 cm) piece of camel-colored wool for the hedgehog's head. Roll the wool into a 1½" (3.8 cm) long cone shape. Use the wooden skewer to help roll the wool tightly and to help make the nose end pointed.

3. Needle the head to help hold the wool in place. Position the head on one end of the gray body and needle the fibers all around the base of the head into the body to attach.

4. Shape the head by needling more at the bridge of the snout and use a darning needle to pull the tip of the snout end out to make it longer and pointed. Wrap a layer of camel-colored wool between the neck area and the body to help create a smooth transition.

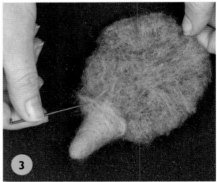

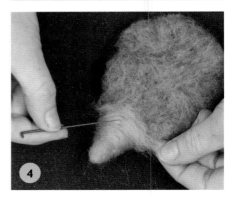

If the head seems too long, stand it up on end on the foam pad. Needle the fibers on the inside by placing the felting needle in the head and punching it without removing the needle all the way out. This is referred to as deep needling.

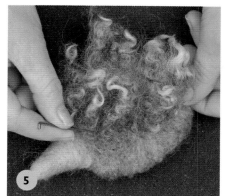

ATTACHING THE CURLY LOCKS

5. Separate the curly locks from each other and observe that one end is the cut end (butt end) and the other end is the curly or loose end. Needle the butt end into the hedgehog's body. You can needle more than just the butt end in if the wool locks seem too long. Cover the whole hedgehog body, but leave the underside without locks.

LEGS

6. Measure a 2" (5.1 cm) long piece of camel-colored wool. Fold it in half and needle it into an oval shape with loose fibers on one end. Make four: two front and two back legs.

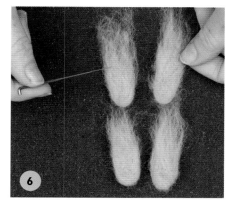

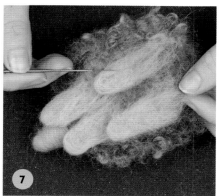

7. Position the legs on the base of the hedgehog. The two front legs should be placed side by side, under the hedgehog's head. The back legs should be placed on either side of the back of the hedgehog, about 1" (2.5 cm) apart.

8. Cover the base with camel-colored wool.

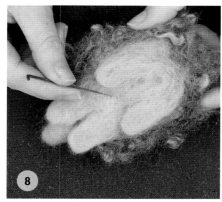

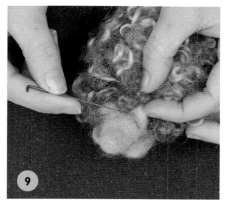

9. To make the ears, fold a 1" (2.5 cm) piece of camel-colored wool in half and needle into a circle. Keep the fibers loose at one end for attaching the ears to the head. Position the ears on each side of the head and needle to attach. Add a curl or two between the ears.

10. Needle a wisp of black wool on the tip of the hedgehog's nose.

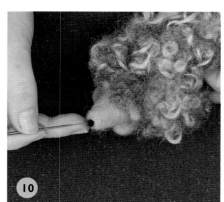

11. Sew beads on each side of the hedgehog's face for eyes.

mushroom
house

This is the perfect little house for wee woodland folks and critters. It's easy to make and fun to decorate with wool felt.

MATERIALS

- 0.15 oz. (5 g) red wool roving
- small amount of white wool roving, preferably merino
- 4" x 6" (10.2 x 15.2 cm) piece of light brown wool felt fabric
- 5" x ¾" (12.7 x 1.9 cm) piece of green felt fabric
- 2" x 2" (5.1 x 5.1 cm) square of blue felt fabric
- embroidery thread and needle
- glue
- scissors
- wool batting or polyfill

FELT HOUSE

1. Fold ½" (1.3cm) at the top and the bottom of the light brown wool and whipstitch or glue.

2. Cut the 2" x 2" (5.1 x 5.1 cm) piece of blue felt in half. Cut one piece in half again, and cut each of those pieces into circles. The rectangle will be the door, the circles the windows.

3. Cut an arc across the top of the door piece. Blanket stitch around the outside edge of the door and sew on a bead for the doorknob.

4. Center the door on the bottom right side of the light brown felt. Glue the door in place.

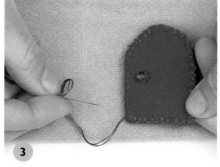

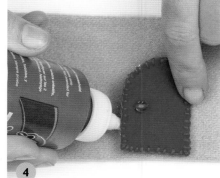

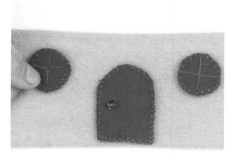

5

5. Blanket stitch around the edges of the windows. Glue the windows to the house.

6. Cut the green strip of wool in half. Snip across the edge to make grass. Glue to the bottom edge of the house.

7. After the glue has dried, whip-stitch the side of the house together.

(continued)

6

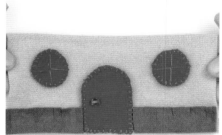

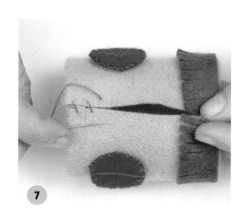

7

MUSHROOM ROOF

8. Measure six 6" (15.2 cm) pieces of red roving. Lay them in a fan shape and needle the fibers together. Turn the piece over and needle the opposite side.

9. Lift up and needle the edges of the roving and shape into an arc.

10. Needle all over the surface to make it smooth.

11. Needle a wisp of white wool into a dot as you are attaching it to the red wool.

12. Cover the red roof with white dots. You can add them randomly or in a pattern.

13. When you are satisfied with the design, fold the right sides of the mushroom roof together and needle down the seam.

14. Turn the mushroom roof inside out and needle the surface to form a cone shape.

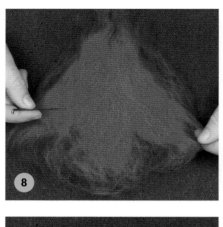
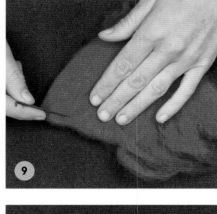
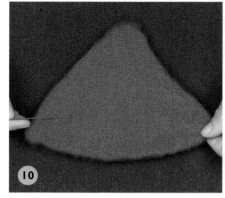
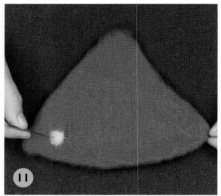
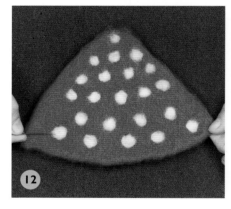
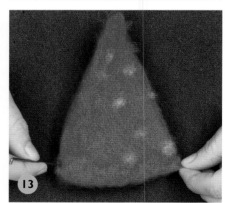

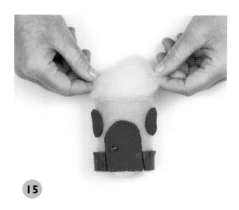

PUTTING IT TOGETHER

15. Roll a piece of batting into a 4" × 2" (10.2 × 5.1 cm) tube. Stuff the tube into the house.

16. Place the roof on top of the house and needle it into the batting enough to keep it from falling off.

starfish beanbags

This starfish beanbag is another easy project to do with children, especially since there is no needle felting involved. You can use any kind of bean for filling, but if there is any chance of the starfish getting wet, it's best to opt for synthetic pellets.

MATERIALS

- 0.5 oz. (14 g) purple wool
- 0.5 oz. (14 g) lavender wool
- two 1-gallon plastic bags
- soap
- spray bottle
- warm water

- towel
- bubble wrap
- marker
- funnel
- lentils or other dry beans
- pattern on page 125

STARFISH

1. Trace the pattern on a piece of plastic bag. Cut the pattern out. Prepare your workspace for wet felting and read the techniques for wet felting on page 14.

2. Cover the pattern with several long, thin layers of purple and lavender wool. Slightly overlap the edges.

3. Spray the wool with warm, soapy water.

4. Cut the gallon-sized plastic bag in two pieces. Lay one piece of the plastic over the wool-covered pattern. Carefully turn the pattern over and fold the wool over the edge of the pattern.

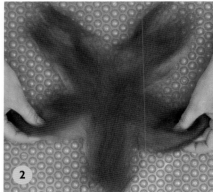

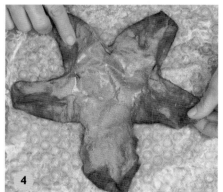

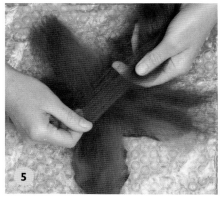

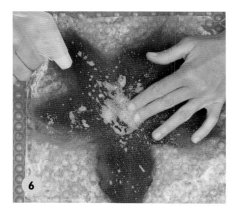

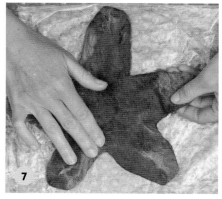

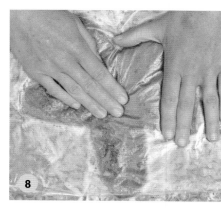

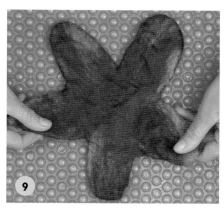

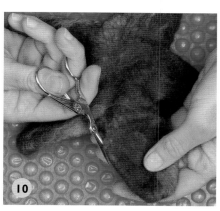

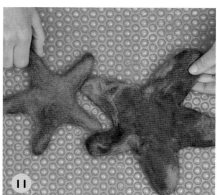

5. Repeat the layering of purple and lavender wool on the pattern.

6. Spray the wool with warm, soapy water.

7. Gently smooth the wool over the surface of the pattern.

8. Cover the wool and pattern with the other piece of plastic bag and rub the surface to begin felting the wool.

9. Turn the piece over and rub for about 15 minutes. Once the wool seems to be holding together well, set the plastic bags aside and rub the starfish directly on the bubble wrap.

10. Cut a slit in the side of the starfish and slide the plastic pattern out.

11. Keep rubbing the starfish until it seems firm. This example shows how much shrinkage should occur before and after felting.

12. Rinse the starfish and let it dry overnight. Once it's dry, use a funnel to fill the body with lentils or other filling.

13. Sew the seam closed.

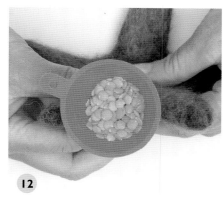

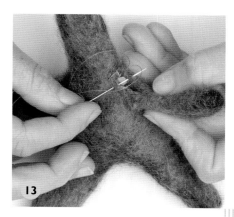

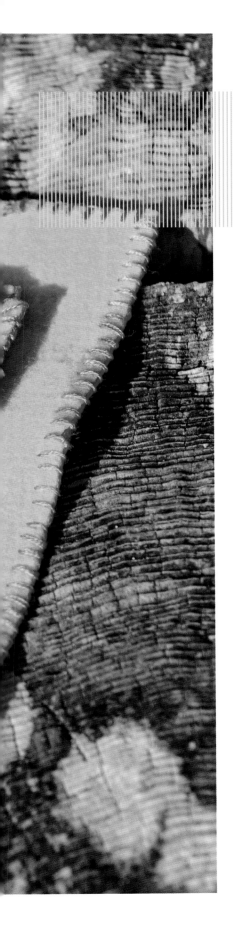

storybook and pocket pals

Children love surprises and this book has sewn-in hiding places for needle-felted friends. Wool felt fabric is wonderful to work with; it's easy to cut and sew, soft to the touch, and comes in many beautiful colors. Holland wool felt is available online and is the best weight for making felt books (see resources for where to buy felt on page 121). Use two strands of embroidery floss unless otherwise noted.

MATERIALS

- 8" x 16" (20.3 x 40.6 cm) piece of yellow wool felt fabric for cover
- two 14" x 6" (35.6 x 15.2 cm) pieces of yellow wool felt fabric for pages
- variety of wool felt fabric scraps in different colors
- small amount of blue, yellow, orange, white, and black wool roving
- scissors
- craft glue
- crewel needle
- felting needle
- foam pad
- ruler
- embroidery floss in complementary colors to felt
- patterns on pages 122, 126–128

THE BOOK

1. Using blue embroidery thread, blanket stitch (page 17) around the border of the book cover and two yellow pages.

2. Layer the two pages and center them over the cover; the cover will extend 1" (2.5 cm) beyond the pages. Use a running stitch to sew the layers together through the center.

3. Turn the book over and check to make sure the stitches are going completely through the three layers of felt.

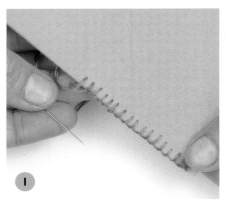

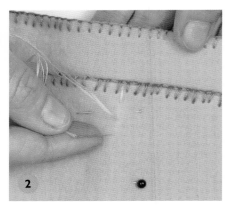

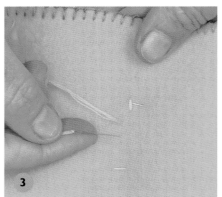

TREE PAGE

4. Cut out all the tree pieces in green felt and the trunk in brown felt. Glue the smaller felt tree-top sections to the larger back tree-top section.

5. Blanket stitch around the edge of the tree using green embroidery floss and stitch around the tree trunk using brown floss. Glue the tree trunk to the first page in the book. Position the tree on the middle of the page and glue just along the edge of the tree, leaving a 3" (7.6 cm) space at the top.

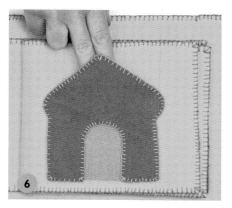

DOG HOUSE PAGE

6. Cut the doghouse out of brown felt. Cut the door shape out of coral felt and glue the edges of the door to the inside curve of the house. After the glue has dried, blanket stitch around the doghouse in coral embroidery floss. Glue the edge of the doghouse to the second page. Leave a 3" (7.6 cm) space open at the top of the house.

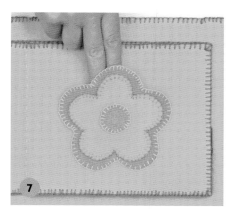

FLOWER PAGE

7. Cut the large flower from coral felt and the smaller flower from yellow felt. Cut the circle out of coral felt. Blanket stitch around the large flower with yellow embroidery floss, the smaller flower with coral embroidery floss, and the center circle with yellow floss. Glue the edge of the flower to the third felt page, leaving a 3" (7.6 cm) opening at the top.

(continued)

WATER PAGE

8. Cut the waves from different shades of blue felt. Blanket stitch along the top edge of each set of waves, using a contrasting color of blue embroidery floss. Glue all three sets of waves together; then glue the outside edge to the fourth page, leaving a 3" (7.6 cm) opening at the top.

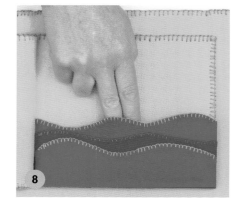

BIRD

9. Measure a 5" × 2" (12.7 × 5.1 cm) piece of blue wool and tightly roll into a 1½" (3.8 cm) long oblong shape that is wide at one end and narrow at the other. Needle all over the surface to help shape the bird's body.

10. Fold a 1" (2.5 cm) long piece of blue wool in half and needle into a flat oval shape for the bird's wing. Make two. Needle the wings to the side of the bird's body.

11. Needle a wisp of black wool on each side of the bird's head for eyes.

12. Needle a wisp of yellow wool on the front of the bird's head for a beak.

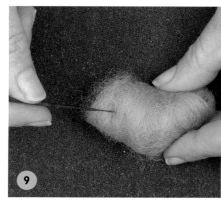

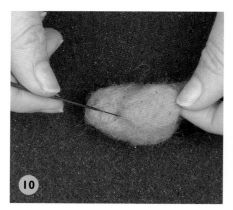

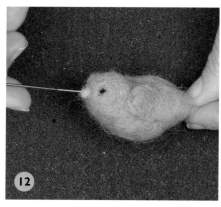

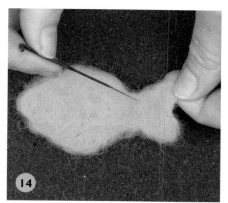

FISH

13. Roll a 5" × 2" (12.7 × 5.1 cm) piece of yellow wool into a 1½" (3.8 cm) diamond shape. Needle to hold the shape.

14. Needle a 2" (5.1 cm) square piece of yellow wool flat and then fold on the diagonal. Needle into a triangle shape for the tail and attach the tail to the fish.

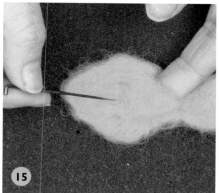

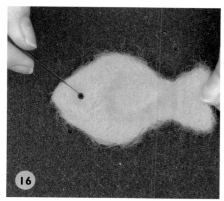

15. Fold a 1" (2.5 cm) long piece of orange wool in half, needle into an arc shape, and attach to the top of the fish for a fin. Make another fin for under the fish's belly.

16. Needle a wisp of black wool into a circle on each side of the fish's head for eyes.

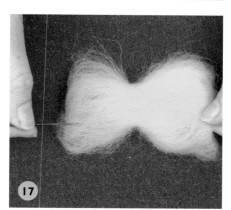

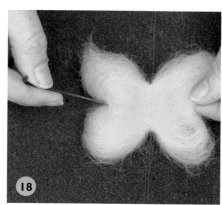

BUTTERFLY

17. Measure a 3" (7.6 cm) square piece of yellow wool and needle it flat. Begin to shape the butterfly's wings by lifting the wool from the middle of the top and bottom of the square and needle toward the center of the square.

18. Hold the middle of the butterfly with one hand and pull the edge out of each corner to help shape the wings.

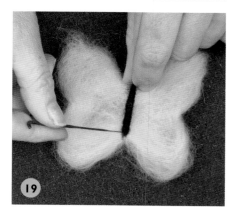

19. Roll a 2" (5.1 cm) long piece of black wool into a thin, 1" (2.5 cm) long tube and needle to the middle of the butterfly's body.

(continued)

DOG

20. Roll a 5" × 2" (12.7 × 5.1 cm) piece of white wool into a 1½" (3.8 cm) long barrel shape. One end should be slightly wider than the other. Needle to hold the shape and smooth the surface.

21. Roll a 3" × 1" (7.6 × 2.5 cm) piece of white wool into a ¾" (1.9 cm) long cone shape. Needle to hold the shape. Position the head on top of the body and needle to attach.

22. To make ears, fold a 1" (2.5 cm) long piece of black wool in half and needle into a small oval shape. Make two ears. Position the ears on each side of the dog's head and needle to attach.

23. Needle a wisp of black wool into a circle on each side of the dog's face for eyes and another wisp on the front of the dog's face for a nose.

24. Fold a 1" (2.5 cm) piece of black wool in half and needle into a tail. Attach the tail to the body.

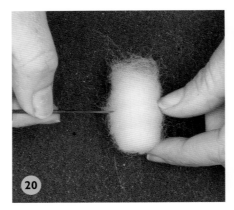
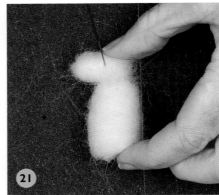

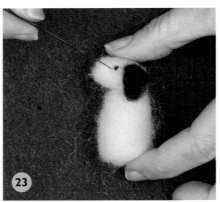
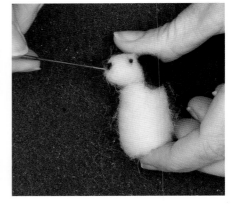

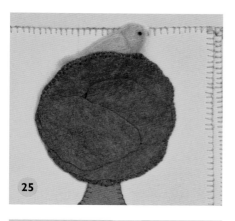

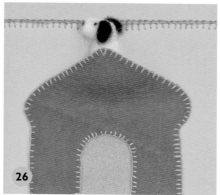

25. Place the needle-felted bird inside the tree.

26. Place the needle-felted dog inside the doghouse.

27. Place the needle-felted butterfly in the flower.

28. Place the needle-felted fish in the waves.

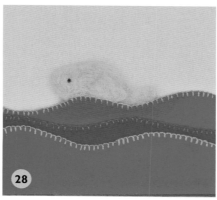

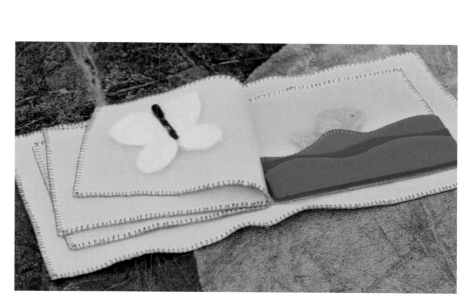

You can sew a ribbon or piece of yarn to each needle-felted animal, and attach the other end to the felt page so that the animals won't get lost. This book may not be appropriate for children under age three because some of the small felt parts can fall off and therefore be a choking hazard.

finger puppets

Finger puppets are easy to make and a joy for children to play with. This is a good project for children to do if an adult helps with the needle felting parts. The instructions show you how to make a sheep, pig, and dog. These patterns can easily be modified to make different finger puppet animals and characters.

MATERIALS

- 0.2 oz (6 g) white wool
- 0.2 oz. (6 g) pink wool
- 0.2 oz (6 g) brown wool
- small handful of curly wool locks
- small amount of dark brown, black, and red wool
- beads for eyes
- felting needle
- felting needle punch or holder
- foam pad

- ruler
- soap
- spray bottle
- warm water
- towel
- bubble wrap
- 4" (10.2 cm) square of acetate or lid from a plastic container
- pattern on page 122

BASIC FINGER PUPPET SHAPES

1. To make a sheep, measure a 7" × 4" (17.8 × 10.2 cm) piece of white wool. Lay it on the foam pad and needle it into a flat, 3" × 5" (7.6 × 12.7 cm) piece. Lift the wool off of the foam pad and needle the other side flat.

2. Fold the wool in half and needle along the edge and up over the top to form a seam.

3. Turn the piece over and needle along the seam to help reinforce it.

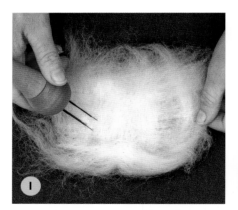

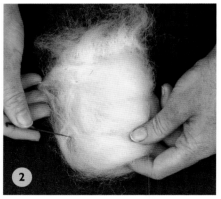

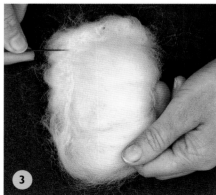

Use a needle punch that holds more than one felting needle to begin making the finger puppet bodies.

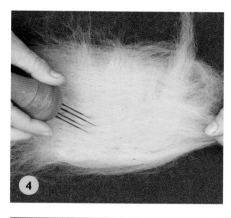

4. To make the pig, repeat steps 1 through 3 with pink wool.

5. To make the dog, repeat steps 1 through 3 with brown wool.

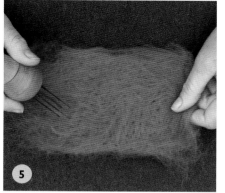

WET FELT THE PUPPETS

6. Trace the template on a piece of acetate or similar piece of plastic. A lid from a take-out container works well, too. Prepare your workspace for wet felting (page 14). Slide the template into the finger puppet sleeve.

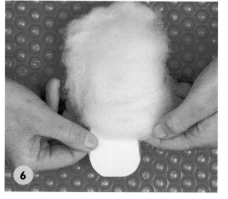

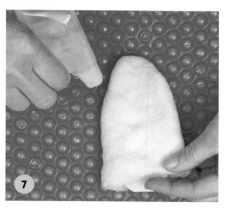

7. Spray the wool with warm, soapy water until it is saturated. Turn the piece over and spray the other side.

8. Gently roll the wetted fibers between your hands until the wool begins to hold to itself. Rub the finger puppet on the bubble wrap with the template inside for about five minutes.

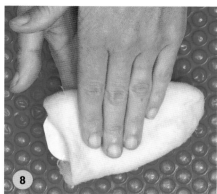

9. Remove the template and continue rolling the wool tube until it seems firm, about another five minutes. Rinse the finger puppet in cold water, squeeze the water out, and allow the puppet to dry overnight.

(continued)

SHEEP

10. To make the sheep's snout, roll a 4" × 1" (10.2 × 2.5 cm) piece of white wool into a 1" (2.5 cm) long cone shape. Needle to help hold the shape. Position the snout on the front of the sheep's face and needle all around the snout to attach.

11. Needle two wisps of white wool into ovals and attach them to either side of the sheep's head for ears.

12. Needle a wisp of pink wool into the middle of the ears.

13. Needle a strip of black wool on the front of the snout to make a mouth.

14. Sew black beads on each side of the head for eyes.

15. Needle the curly wool locks all over the body.

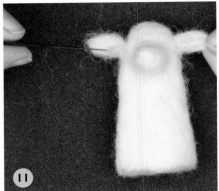

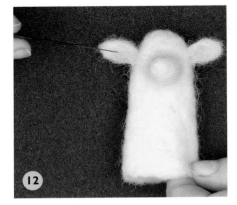

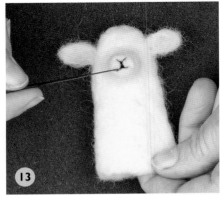

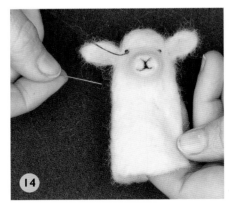

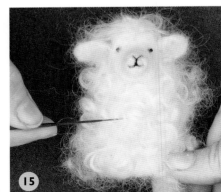

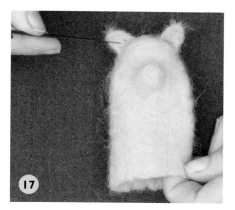

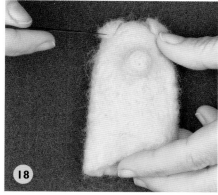

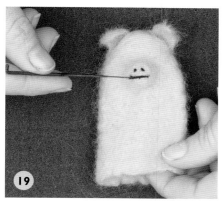

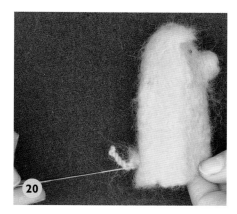

PIG

16. Needle a small pink ball on the front of the pig's face for a snout.

17. Take two wisps of pink wool and needle them into triangles. Attach the ears to the top of the pig's head.

18. Fold the ears down and needle in place.

19. Needle two dots of black wool on the pig's snout and a thin line under the dots.

20. Twist a small piece of pink wool in your fingers and needle it to the back of the pig to make a curly tail.

21. Sew black beads on each side of the pig's head for eyes.

(continued)

While attaching the snout, check occasionally that the finger puppet still has a hollow space in the middle and that the tube is open by inserting a finger and separating the fibers.

DOG

22. To make the dog's snout, repeat step 10 for making the sheep snout. Use brown wool instead of white.

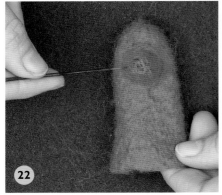

23. Needle a small, flat oval-shaped piece of brown wool underneath the snout to make a mouth.

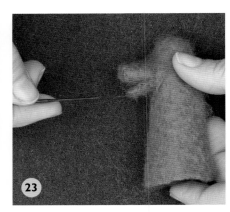

24. Needle a dot of black wool on the front of the dog's snout for a nose. Needle a thin line of black wool under the nose and down the snout.

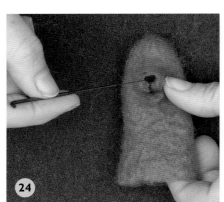

25. Needle a wisp of red wool on the dog's mouth for a tongue.

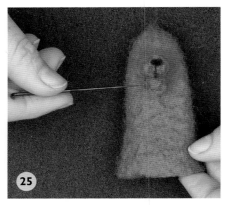

26. To make eyes, needle two white circles of wool on the dog's face, then black circles of wool within the white.

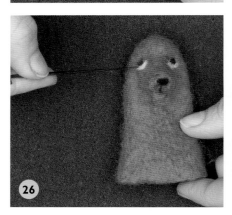

27. Needle a speck of white wool inside the black circles.

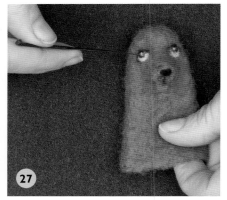

28. Needle two pieces of dark brown wool into small oval shapes. Attach the ears to either side of the dog's head.

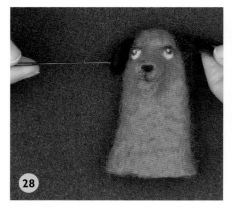

29. Roll a wisp of dark brown wool into a small cone shape and needle it on the back of the dog for a tail.

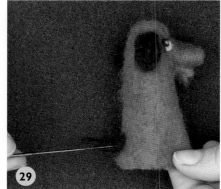

lion hand puppet

This lion hand puppet is made using both wet felting and needle felting techniques. Most of the puppet is wet felted around a template. The details on the lion's face and his mane are needle felted. This pattern can be adapted to make other animal hand puppets. Try making a dog, cat, or sheep.

MATERIALS

- 0.75 oz. (21 g) gold wool
- 0.5 oz. (14 g) toffee wool
- small amount of white, black, and brown wool
- felting needle
- foam pad
- two 1-gallon sealable plastic bags
- soap

- marker
- scissors
- spray bottle
- warm water
- bubble wrap
- towel
- pattern on page 123

THE PUPPET

Before you begin to make the puppet, review the techniques for wet felting (page 14).

1. Using a black marker, trace the puppet pattern on one side of the plastic bag. Cut out the pattern and cut the other plastic bag in half so that you have three squares of plastic. Prepare your work surface for wet felting. Lay out a towel, bubble wrap, and the pattern. Fill the spray bottle with warm, soapy water and set it nearby.

2. Cover one half of the puppet template with wool by tearing wisps apart from the roving and laying them in the same direction; then create another layer going in the opposite direction. Repeat with one more crisscross layer of wool.

3. Spray the entire wool surface with warm, soapy water.

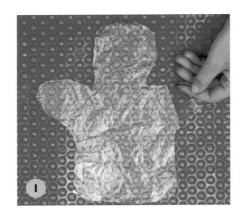

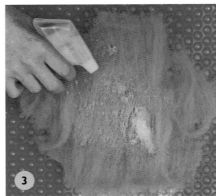

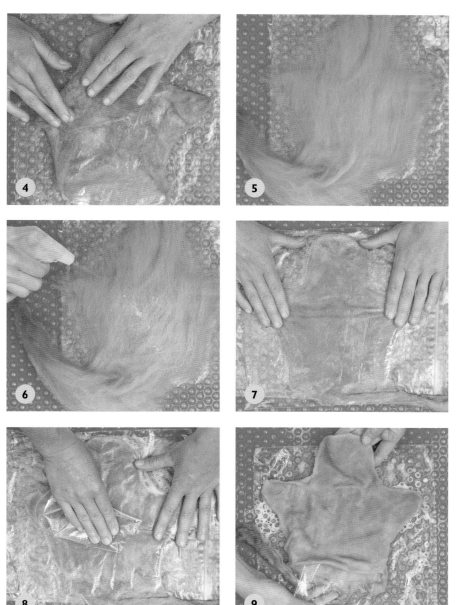

4. Lay a square of plastic over the wetted wool and gently rub the surface. Turn the piece over.

5. Repeat the cross-layering of the roving on the template. The tail will also be made now. Lay wisps of gold roving in a line starting at the middle of the bottom edge of the puppet. Add a few wisps of toffee wool at the end of the gold wool. You should have 12" (30.5 cm) of roving laid out for the tail.

6. Spray to wet the wool.

7. Lay a piece of plastic over the wetted wool. You should have a "sandwich" as follows: plastic, wool, template, wool, plastic, bubble wrap, and a towel underneath all of it.

8. With the third piece of plastic, gently rub the wool. Make sure the wool is evenly wet and spray more soapy water if needed.

9. Turn the puppet over again and rub the wool for approximately 15 minutes. When the wool seems to have a shell, remove the plastic and begin to rub with more pressure.

   Insert your hand inside the puppet and remove the template. Turn the puppet inside out and rub the puppet on the bubble wrap.

(continued)

10. Roll the tail between your palms to help make it into a cord.

11. Keep rubbing the puppet on the bubble wrap and turn it right side out. When the wool seems to be well felted, rinse the puppet in cool water and roll it in a towel. Let the puppet dry overnight or longer if necessary. The photo shows how much shrinkage occurs during the felting process.

NEEDLE FELTED DETAILS

12. Once the puppet is dry, the details will be directly needle felted on the face and head.

13. Roll and needle three small white balls on the front of the lion's face for a muzzle.

14. Needle a flat piece of gold wool on the top of the muzzle to make the bridge of the lion's nose.

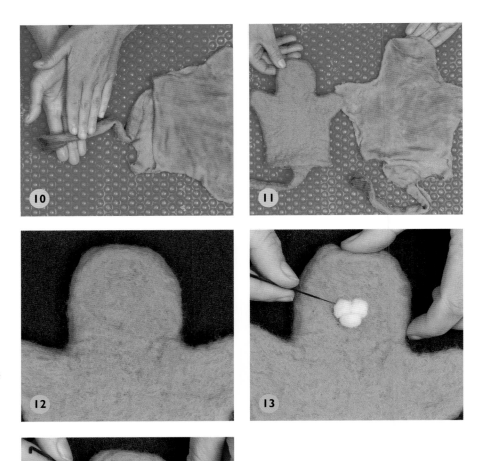

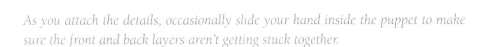

As you attach the details, occasionally slide your hand inside the puppet to make sure the front and back layers aren't getting stuck together.

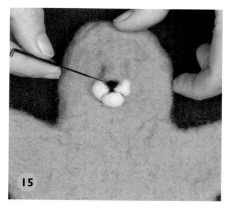

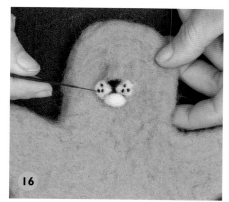

15. Needle a black triangle on the tip of the bridge for a nose. Needle a line of black wool from the nose down and split it in half. Needle each half along the bottom of the muzzle.

16. Needle a few dots of black wool on the muzzle.

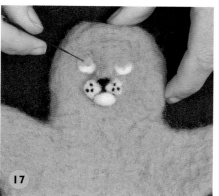

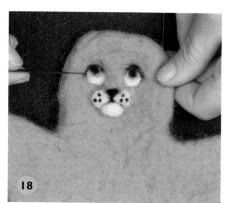

EYES

17. Needle two circles of white wool on the lion's face for eyes. Needle a circle of gold wool within the white circle.

18. Needle a circle of brown wool inside of the gold.

19. Needle a speck of white inside of the brown.

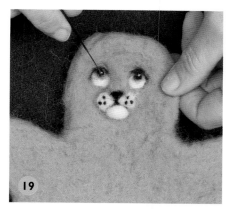

EARS

20. Measure a 2" × 1" (5.1 × 2.5 cm) piece of gold wool. Needle the wool into a 1" (2.5 cm) wide circle. Make two ears. Position the ears on either side of the lion's head and needle to attach.

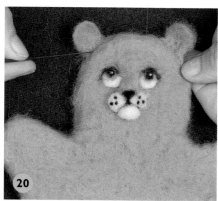

(continued)

MANE

21. Lay a 3" (7.6 cm) long strip of toffee wool perpendicular to the lion's face, under the muzzle. Needle the middle of the strip.

22. Fold the strip in half and needle down to lock the fibers in place.

23. Repeat laying down the wool strips, needling the middle, and folding in half until the front of the lion's head is covered.

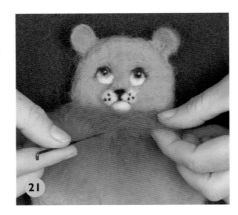

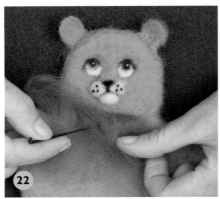

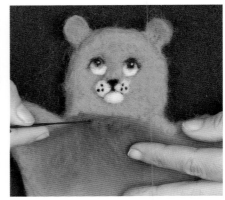

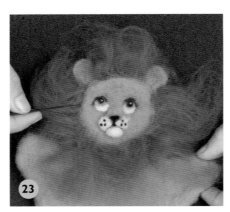

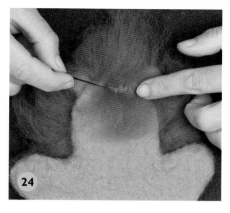

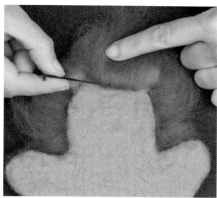

24. Add strips of toffee roving to the back of the lion's head. Starting just below the mane, needle a row of 3" (7.6 cm) long toffee wisps. Fold the wisps in half and needle the middle of the strip, the same way you created the mane in front.

25. Make sure the mane looks full and even. Attach more toffee wool if needed.

matryoshka doll

Matryoshka dolls are also known as nesting dolls. Traditionally, they are made out of wood with painted details and come in sets— a large doll with increasingly smaller dolls nested inside of each other. This needle-felted version can be made into a set of different sizes to resemble the traditional dolls. These instructions make a 4" (10.2 cm) doll.

MATERIALS

- 0.15 oz. (5 g) flesh-colored wool
- 0.35 oz. (10 g) blue wool
- 0.15 oz. (5 g) yellow wool
- small amount of white, black, green, red, and dark brown wool

- felting needle
- foam pad
- ruler

HEAD AND FACE

1. Measure a 2" × 8" (5.1 × 20.3 cm) piece of flesh-colored wool and tightly roll into a 1" (2.5 cm) wide ball. Needle the surface to help keep the fibers from unrolling.

2. Needle a groove across the middle of the face. This will be a guide to help with positioning the eyes and nose, and help shape the face.

3. Roll a wisp of flesh-colored wool into a ball. Needle it on the middle of the face for a nose.

4. Needle a wisp of white wool on each side of the doll's face for eyes.

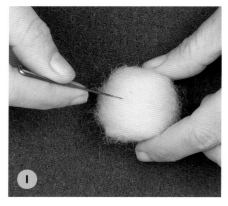

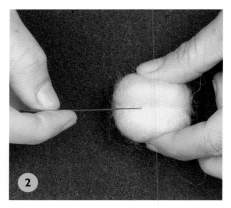

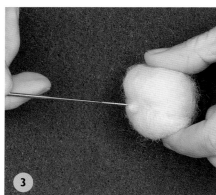

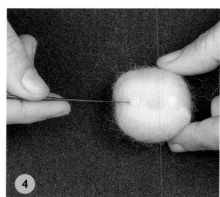

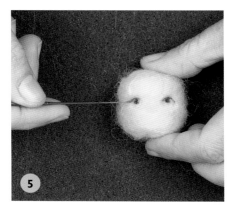

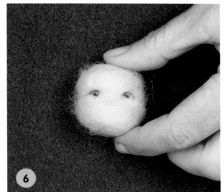

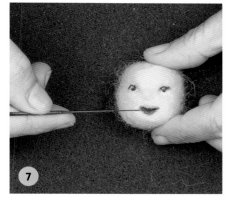

5. Needle a wisp of black wool within the white eye.

6. Needle a speck of white wool in the black wool of the eye. Needle a wisp of black wool along the top of the eye for an eye line.

7. Needle a piece of black wool under the nose for a mouth. Roll a wisp of red wool just slightly and needle it under the black wool. Needle the edges of the red up so that the doll appears to be smiling.

(continued)

DOLL BODY

8. Measure a 2" × 12" (5.1 × 30.5 cm) piece of blue wool and roll it into a 2½" (6.4 cm) long barrel shape.

9. Choose which end of the body will be the base. Turn the base end up and needle it flat so that the doll can stand.

10. To make the arms, needle two 1" × 2" (2.5 × 5.1 cm) pieces of blue wool flat. Fold these in half lengthwise and needle. Narrow the shape of the arms by lifting the sides and needling them toward the middle.

11. Position the arms on the sides of the body and needle all around the edge of the arm and into the body to attach.

12. Needle a wisp of flesh-colored wool into a ball and attach it to the wrist of each arm to make hands.

13. Position the head on top of the body and needle all around the edge of the head and into the body to attach.

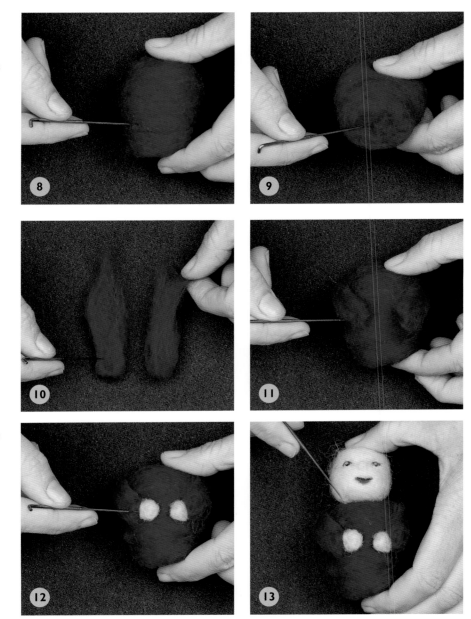

SCARF

14. Measure a 7" × 1" (17.8 × 2.5 cm) piece of yellow wool. Separate the layers of wool and lay them out in a triangle shape on the foam pad. Needle the wool flat. Turn the triangle over and needle the opposite side.

15. Lay the scarf over the doll's head and tie the corners under the chin. Needle the edge of the scarf all around the doll's head. Needle around the bottom edge of the scarf into the doll's body.

16. Continue needling the scarf until it looks smooth and shows the outline of the head. Needle it at the back of the head so that it looks curved.

17. Needle a few curls of dark brown wool along the doll's hairline.

DETAILS

18. Be creative with the details on the doll. Using very small amounts of wool, needle colorful patterns, trims, and decorations on the doll's body and scarf. Needle a bit of bunched-up wool into her hands for a flower. Or, needle a heart for the doll to hold.

To make other sizes of dolls, adjust the amount of wool used and the size of the head, body, and arms.

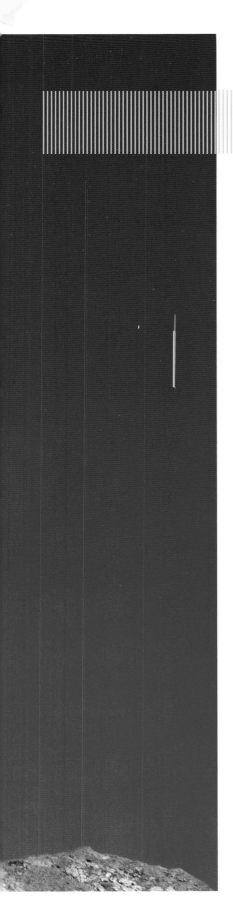

dala horse

The name "Dala" comes from a village in Sweden called Dalarna where the charming little horses were made from scraps of wood left over from the clock case industry. This wool version is made by combining needle and wet felting, and it is "painted" with wisps of merino wool.

MATERIALS

- 0.5 oz. (14 g) red wool
- small amount of white, yellow, green, and orange merino wool
- darning needle
- soap
- spray bottle
- warm water
- wooden skewer
- felting needle
- foam pad
- ruler
- towel

BODY

1. Measure an 8" × 2" (20.3 × 5.1 cm) piece of red wool and tightly roll into a 3" × 1" (7.6 × 2.5 cm) barrel shape.

2. Add another layer of red wool and needle the surface to help keep the fiber from unrolling.

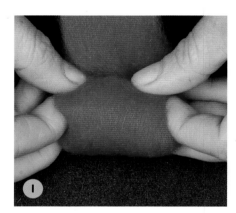
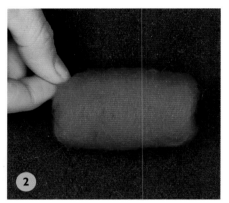

NECK/HEAD

3. Measure a 6" × 2" (15.2 × 5.1 cm) piece of red wool and roll into a 1½" (3.8 cm) cone. Needle the surface all around to help keep the fibers in place.

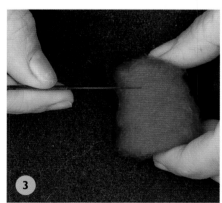

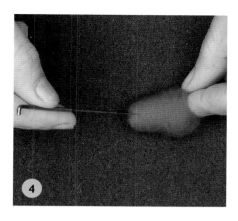

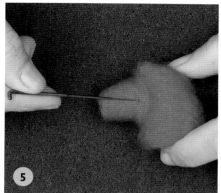

MUZZLE

4. Needle a 4" × 1" (10.2 × 2.5 cm) piece of red wool into a 1" × ½" (2.5 × 1.3 cm) cone.

5. Position the muzzle on the head/ neck piece and needle all around the edge of the muzzle into the head to attach.

6. Cover the area of attachment with a wisp of red wool to help smooth out any lines. Needle to help form a strong attachment.

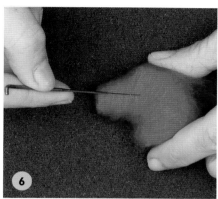

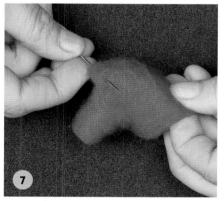

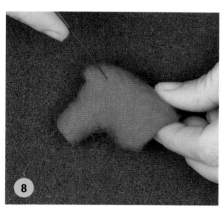

EARS

7. Insert the darning needle at the top of the horse's head and gently pull the wool up to form the ears.

8. Needle all around the ears to help form the shape.

9. Position the head and neck on top of the body and needle all around the base of the neck into the body to attach.

10. Needle a wisp of red wool around the area of attachment so that it looks smooth.

(continued)

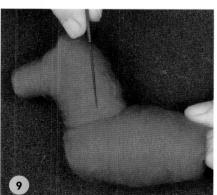

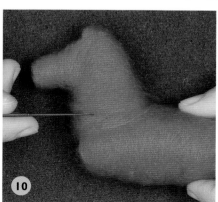

LEGS

11. Review the techniques for making needle felted legs (page 13). Tightly roll a 6" × 1" (15.2 × 2.5 cm) piece of red wool into a 2" (5.1 cm) long leg shape.

12. Make three more legs.

13. Position a leg on one side of the horse's body and needle to attach.

14. Attach the other three legs; then add some more red wool around the area of attachment to increase the stability of the legs. Needle the wool to help smooth the surface.

15. Fill a small spray bottle with warm, soapy water. Place a towel under the horse and lightly spray all over the horse's body. Gently massage the wet, soapy wool until a "skin" is formed on the surface. Pat the surface dry with the towel and allow the horse to dry before continuing on to the next steps.

16. When the horse is dry, make sure that the legs are even and needle to make any necessary adjustments in the body shape.

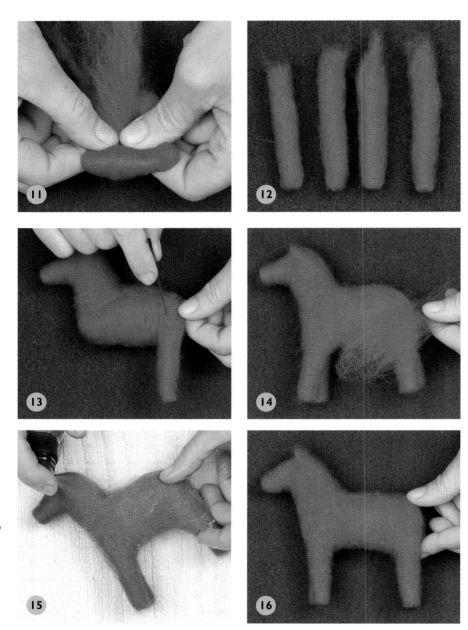

You don't need to spray the horse until it is soaking wet. If you are having trouble massaging the surface with your bare hands, wear a plastic bag over your hand so that you can "glide" more over the surface. It can take up to 30 minutes of rubbing to get a smooth skin on the surface.

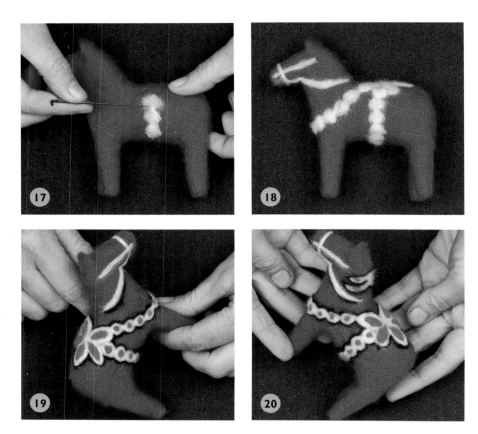

17. Refer to a photo of the patterns painted on a Dala horse and begin adding the details. Starting with the white merino, use the smallest amount of wool to needle the design onto the surface.

18. Use white merino wool to make a flower-shaped saddle and reins.

19. Outline the white wool with green merino wool. Needle orange wool into the center of each white circle and in the middle of the flower on the horse's back.

20. Needle some yellow wool on the back of the horse's neck to make a mane. Outline the yellow wool with green wool.

You only need to use a small amount of wool to create the details, and you don't need to needle very deeply into the horse. Remember, you are trying to achieve a painted look.

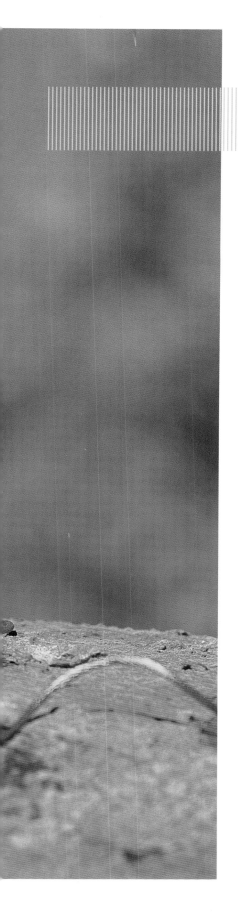

elephant pull toy

Pull toys are a favorite for young children who love to pull things along, taking their treasured pets on journeys near and far. The wooden wheels and string attached to this needle-felted elephant give it additional heirloom quality.

MATERIALS

- 0.5 oz. (14 g) gray wool
- small amount of white and black wool
- felting needle
- foam pad
- ruler
- four 1" (2.5 cm) round wooden wheels

- four ¼" (6 mm) round wooden beads
- red acrylic paint
- small paintbrush
- craft glue
- 48" (122 cm) long piece of red satin ribbon
- two 4" (10.2 cm) wooden skewers

BODY

1. Tightly roll a 16" x 2½" (40.6 x 6.4 cm) piece of gray wool into a 4" x 2" (10.2 x 5.1 cm) tube shape. Needle the surface to help hold the shape.

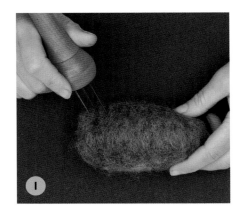

HEAD

2. Tightly roll a 16" (40.6 cm) piece of gray wool into a 2" (5.1 cm) round ball and needle the surface to help keep the ball from unrolling.

3. Position the head on one end of the body. Needle the fibers from the head into the body to attach. Add extra wool around the neck area, and needle to help form a smooth attachment.

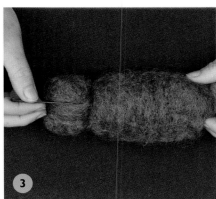

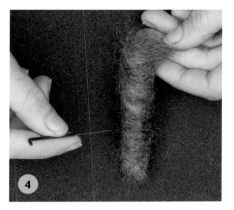

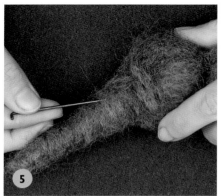

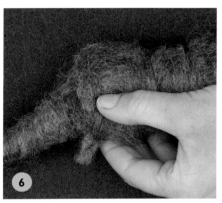

TRUNK

4. Use the skewer to tightly roll a 12" × 1" (30.5 × 2.5 cm) piece of gray wool into a 3½" (8.9 cm) long trunk. Keep the fibers loose at one end to attach the trunk to the head.

5. Position the loose fibers of the trunk on the front of the elephant's head and needle to attach. Cover the area of attachment with a layer of fibers and needle all around the trunk to make it look smooth.

6. Needle a small piece of gray wool into an oval shape and attach it under the trunk for a chin.

LEGS

7. Use the skewer to tightly roll a 9" × 2" (22.9 × 5.1 cm) piece of gray wool into a 3" (7.6 cm) long leg. Keep the fibers loose at one end and needle the fibers in at the other end to make a flat foot.

8. Make three more legs the same way.

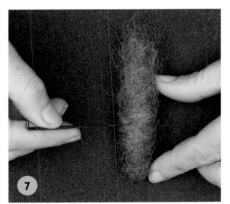

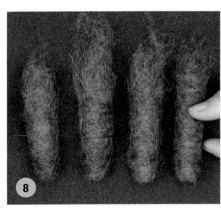

ATTACHING THE LEGS TO THE BODY

9. Position the loose fibers of the legs onto the side of the elephant's body and needle to attach.

10. Add a layer of gray wool around the area of attachment so the elephant can stand on sturdy legs. Pad the area with wool and needle until it looks smooth.

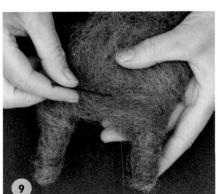

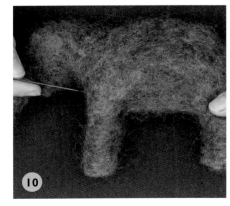

(continued)

EARS

11. Needle a 2" (5.1 cm) piece of gray wool into a flat oval shape. Gently lift the wool off of the foam pad and needle the back. Shape the ear by lifting the fibers from the edge of the ear toward the center. Keep the fibers loose at one end to help attach the ear to the head. Make two ears.

12. Position the ears on either side of the head and needle the loose fibers of the ears into the head to attach.

13. Gently push the ears toward the back of the head and needle the inside of the ears to help form a secure attachment.

14. Needle a wisp of white wool into the middle part of each ear.

EYES

15. Needle a small wisp of white wool into a circle on each side of the elephant's head. Needle a smaller black circle within the white.

16. Needle a tiny white speck in the black circle.

TAIL

17. Roll a 3" (7.6 cm) long piece of gray wool into a long, thin shape. Leave the fibers loose at one end and attach the tail to the back of the elephant.

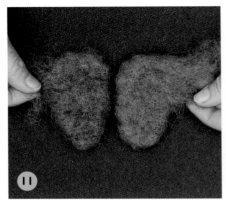

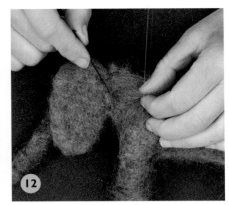

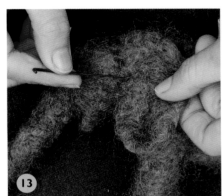

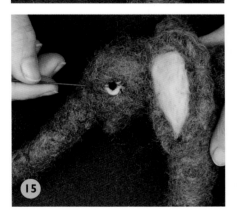

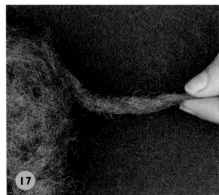

PULL FRAME

18. Paint the wooden skewers, beads, and wheels with red acrylic paint and allow all the parts to dry overnight.

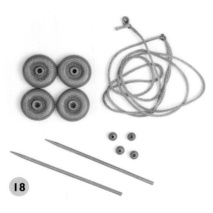

19. Gently twist the pointy end of the skewer into the bottom part of the elephant's leg. Twist the skewer all the way through to the opposite leg and out. Repeat with the back leg and other wooden skewer.

20. Place the wooden wheels on the end of the skewers. You might need to twist the wheels on to make them fit. Glue the wooden beads on the end of the skewer so that the wheels roll freely and won't slide off.

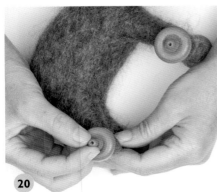

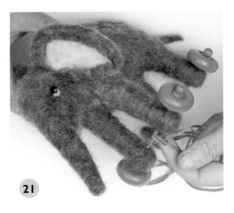

21. Tie the red ribbon on the front skewer and the elephant is ready to roll!

sock monkey

Sock monkeys are a charming reminder that even something as ordinary as a sock can be transformed into a soft plaything. This woolly, needle-felted version is easy and fun to make.

MATERIALS

- 0.5 oz. (14 g) gray wool
- small amount of white and red wool
- felting needle
- foam pad

- ruler
- wooden skewer
- darning needle
- black beads for eyes

BODY

1. Tightly roll a 7" × 2" (17.8 × 5.1 cm) piece of gray wool into a 2" × 1½" (5.1 × 3.8 cm) long barrel shape. Needle the shape to keep the fibers from unrolling.

HEAD

2. Roll a 5" × 1" (12.7 × 2.5 cm) piece of gray wool into a 1" (2.5 cm) wide ball. Needle the surface to help keep the fibers in place.

3. Position the head on top of the body and needle to attach.

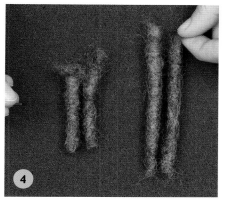

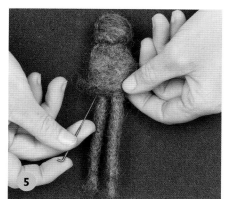

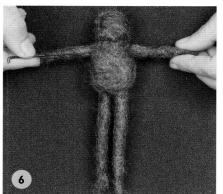

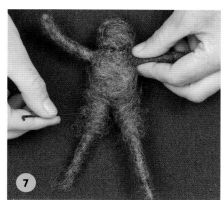

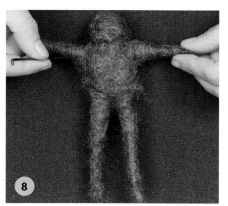

ARMS AND LEGS

4. Measure a 5" × 1" (12.7 × 2.5 cm) piece of gray wool and use the wooden skewer to tightly roll it into a 4" (10.2 cm) long leg. Keep the fibers loose at one end to help attach the leg to the body. Make two legs. Measure a 3" × 1" (7.6 × 2.5 cm) piece of gray wool. Use the skewer to help tightly roll the wool into a 2½" (6.4 cm) long arm. Keep the fibers loose at one end to help attach the arm to the body. Make two arms.

5. Position the legs on the bottom of the sock monkey's body and needle the loose fibers into the body to attach.

6. Position the arms on either side of the sock monkey's body and needle the loose fibers into the body to attach.

7. Wrap a thin layer of gray wool around the area of attachment between the legs and body. Do not wrap tightly. Needle the wool around the attachment so that it looks smooth.

8. Wrap a thin layer of gray wool around the arms at the shoulder and needle to help smooth out the attachment between the arms and body.

(continued)

EARS

9. For ears, needle a wisp of gray wool into a ½" (1.3 cm) circle. Make two.

10. Position the ears on either side of the monkey's head and needle to attach.

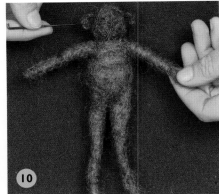

DETAILS

11. Wrap white wool around the end of the legs and arms. Needle the wool to help keep the fibers from unrolling.

12. Needle the fibers at the bottom of each arm and leg so they look smooth and rounded.

13. Needle a ball of white wool on the monkey's face to make the mouth.

14. Needle a strip of red wool across the middle of the mouth. Use the darning needle to help pull the mouth back into shape if it gets flattened.

15. Wrap a thin strip of red wool around the white parts on the arms and legs.

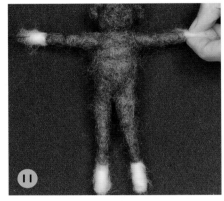

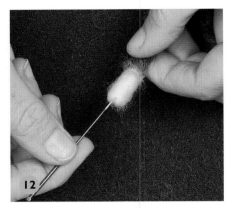

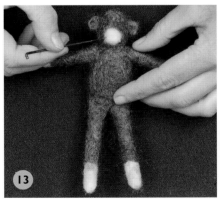

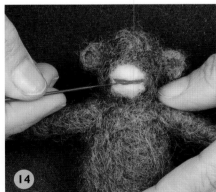

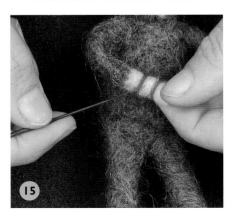

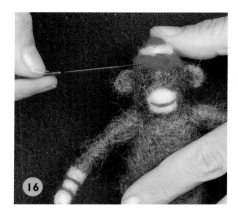

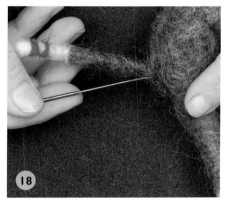

HAT

16. Needle a red cap on the top of the monkey's head. Add a white stripe to the middle of the hat. Use the darning needle to pull up at the top of the hat.

17. Sew black beads on the monkey's face for eyes.

18. Make a tail in the same shape and size as the legs. Needle the loose fibers into the bottom of the monkey. Add details to the tail.

mouse in
pumpkin

This is a great project to try if you'd like to learn how to make a hollow felted vessel. The mouse in a pumpkin is sure to charm people young and old.

MATERIALS

- 0.75 oz. (21 g) orange wool
- 0.50 oz. (14 g) apricot wool
- 0.25 oz. (7 g) white wool
- small amount of green, light green, black, and pink wool
- felting needle
- foam pad
- two round balloons

- old pair of nylon knee-high pantyhose
- soap
- scissors
- spray bottle
- warm water
- bubble wrap
- towel

PUMPKIN

1. Prepare your work area for wet felting. Review the techniques for wet felting (page 14). Separate the orange roving into several long, thin strips, each about 8" (20.3 cm) long. Arrange the strips in several layers like spokes on a wheel. Slightly overlap the strips of wool.

2. Repeat with the apricot wool, but make the circle slightly smaller than the orange one.

3. Lay the apricot wool on top of the orange wool and spray the surface with warm, soapy water. You don't need to get the wool totally soaked. This will to hold the wool together as you wrap it around the balloon and begin the felting process.

4. Fill the balloon with air until it measures about 8" (20.3 cm) in diameter. Place the balloon on the middle of the wool pile and gently fold the wool up around the sides of the balloon. Spray the wool with warm, soapy water to help it stick to the balloon.

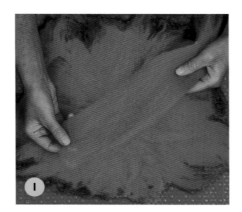

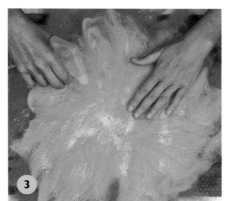

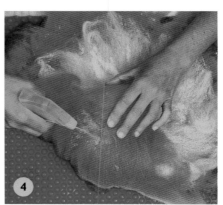

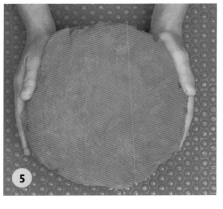

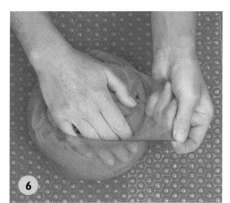

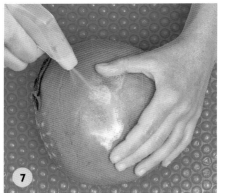

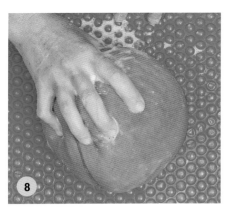

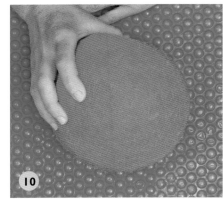

5. Cover the whole balloon with the wool. This might take a bit of practice and time, but be patient and it will work.

6. Stretch the nylon stocking wide enough to place the wool-covered balloon inside. It might help to have another person hold the stocking open while you place the woolly balloon inside.

7. Spray the nylon ball with warm, soapy water until it is saturated.

8. Gently rub the ball on the bubble wrap. Rub the whole surface in different directions. This will help the wool to felt. You can rub harder as the wool gets firmer.

9. After 15 minutes of rubbing, remove the nylon stocking.

10. Rub the wool-covered balloon on the bubble wrap until the surface seems tight and smooth.

(continued)

11. Cut a small opening in the ball, pop the balloon, and remove it.

12. Roll the pumpkin around in your hands to help make it firmer.

13. When the pumpkin seems very firm, fill the inside with another blown-up balloon and let it dry overnight or longer if necessary.

14. After the pumpkin is dry, remove the balloon and stitch the opening closed.

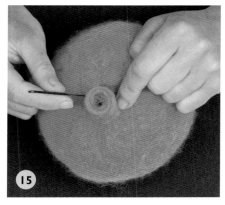

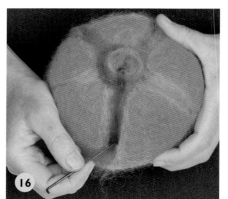

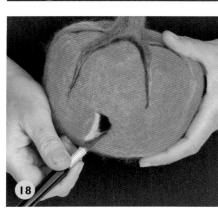

STEM

15. Roll a 5" × 2" (12.7 × 5.1 cm) piece of light green wool into a short tube and needle it to the top of the pumpkin. Needle the stem directly over the spot where the opening is stitched closed.

16. Lay wisps of light green and green wool down the sides of the pumpkin and needle them to attach.

17. Layer wisps of light green and green wool on the stem and continue down the sides of the pumpkin. Needle to attach.

18. Cut a small opening in the side of the pumpkin.

(continued)

MOUSE

19. Tightly roll a 6" × 2" (15.2 × 5.1 cm) piece of white wool into a 2½" (6.4 cm) cone shape. Needle the surface to help keep the shape.

20. Needle two small circles of white wool to make the mouse's ears. Leave the fibers loose at one end to help attach the ears to the mouse.

21. Position the ears on the top of the mouse's head and needle to attach.

22. Roll a 3" (7.6 cm) piece of white wool into a thin strip for the mouse's tail. Leave the fibers loose at one end and needle the tail to the back of the mouse.

23. Needle two small black dots of wool on each side of the mouse's head for eyes.

24. Needle a pink dot of wool on the tip of the mouse's face for a nose. Needle a thin wisp of black wool under the nose to make a mouth.

25. Needle a wisp of pink wool inside of the mouse's ears.

26. Hide the mouse inside the pumpkin!

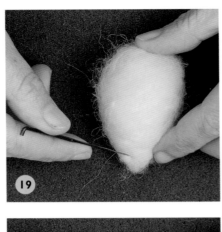

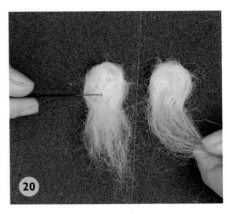

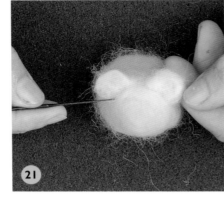

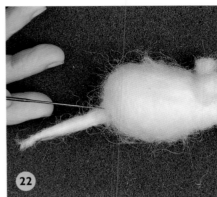

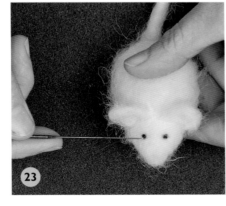

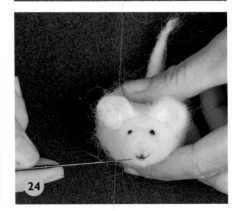

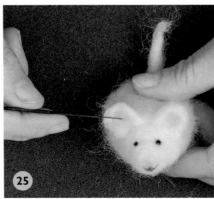

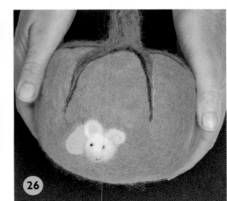

teddy bear

This toy-making book would not be complete without a teddy bear. Wool is very soft and warm to the touch, making this needle-felted bear a snuggly delight.

MATERIALS

- 0.5 oz. (14 g) gold wool
- small amount of white and dark brown wool
- felting needle
- foam pad
- ruler

BODY

1. Tightly roll an 18" × 4" (45.7 × 10.2 cm) piece of gold wool into a 5" × 4" (12.7 × 10.2 cm) egg shape. Needle to help hold the shape and keep the fibers from unrolling.

HEAD

2. Tightly roll a 12" × 2" (30.5 × 5.1 cm) piece of gold wool into a 3" (7.6 cm) round ball and needle to hold the shape.

3. Position the head on top of the body and needle to attach.

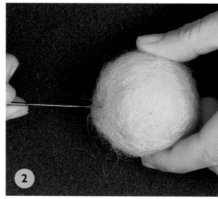
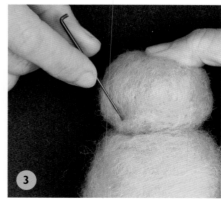

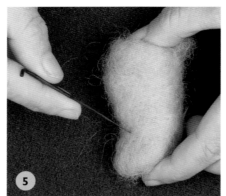

LEGS AND ARMS

4. Tightly roll a 12" × 2" (30.5 × 5.1 cm) piece of gold wool into a 4" (10.2 cm) long tube shape. Keep the fibers loose at one end.

5. To help shape the foot, needle an indentation at the instep.

6. Needle a groove behind the knee on the leg.

7. Repeat to make a second leg.

8. The arms are made similarly to the legs. Tightly roll a 10" × 1" (25.4 × 2.5 cm) piece of gold wool into a 3½" (8.9 cm) long tube shape. Keep the fibers loose at one end to help attach the arms to the body.

9. Repeat to make a second arm.

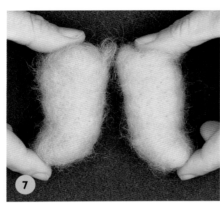

(continued)

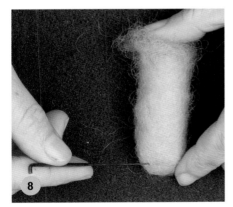

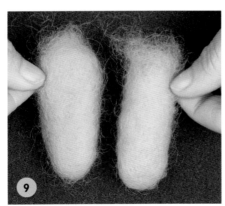

10. Position the legs on either side of the bear's body and needle to attach.

11. The bear's legs are positioned so that the bear can sit up.

12. Position the arms on the bear's body, just above the legs, and needle to attach.

13. Make sure the arms and legs are securely attached and evenly spaced.

14. Wrap an extra layer of wool around the area of attachment between the legs and body and needle until it looks smooth.

15. Wrap an extra layer of wool around the arms, head, and neck area. Needle so that the areas of attachment look smooth.

16. Bring some extra wool from the neck up and around the head. Needle the wool smooth.

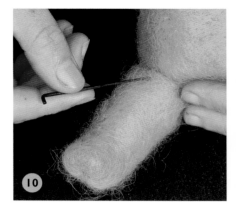
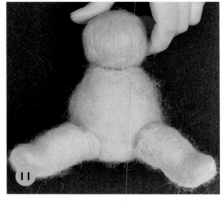
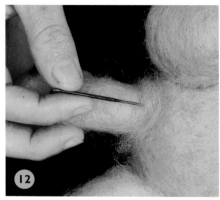
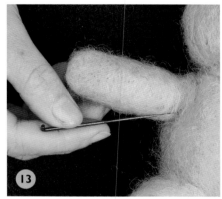
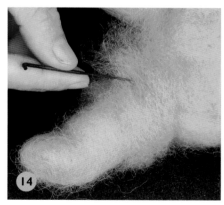
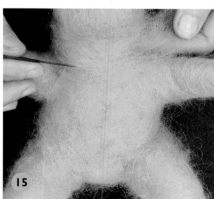
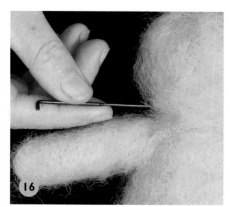

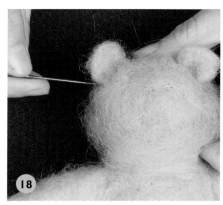

EARS

17. Needle two wisps of gold wool into ¾" (1.9 cm) round circles. Leave the fibers loose at one end to help attach the ears to the head.

18. Position the ears on either side of the bear's head and needle to attach.

(continued)

FACE DETAILS

19. Roll a 3" (7.6 cm) piece of gold wool into a ¾" (1.9 cm) ball and needle it to the front of the bear's face for a snout.

20. Needle a small ½" (1.3 cm) disc of gold wool underneath the snout for a mouth.

21. Needle a wisp of dark brown wool on the tip of the snout for a nose. Needle a line of dark brown wool underneath the nose.

22. Needle two circles of white wool on the bear's face for eyes.

23. Needle a smaller circle of dark brown within each white circle.

24. Needle a speck of white inside of each dark brown circle.

25. Layer some gold wool on the bear's tummy and needle it smooth and round.

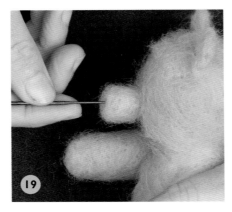

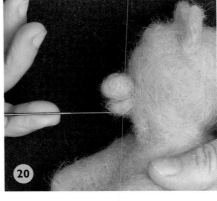

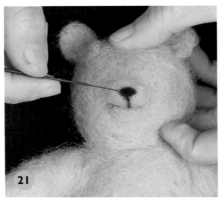

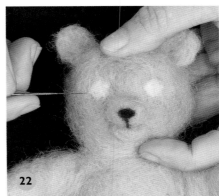

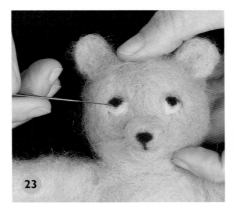

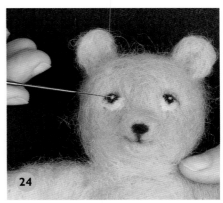

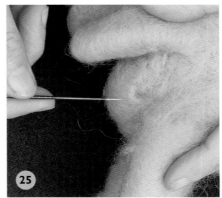

japanese doll

Gift giving is pervasive in Japanese culture and simple handcrafted dolls are a common gift. This needle-felted doll will be a welcome addition to any doll lover's collection.

MATERIALS

- 0.2 oz. (6 g) flesh-colored wool
- 0.4 oz. (11 g) orange wool
- 0.2 oz. (6 g) gold wool
- small amount of white and black wool
- black beads for eyes
- felting needle
- foam pad
- ruler

HEAD AND FACE

1. Measure a 2" x 8" (5.1 x 20.3 cm) piece of flesh-colored wool and tightly roll into a 1" (2.5 cm) wide ball. Needle the surface to help keep the fibers from unrolling.

2. Roll a wisp of flesh-colored wool into a ball and needle it onto the middle of the doll's face for a nose.

3. Needle two wisps of white wool on the doll's face for eyes.

4. Sew black beads inside of the white circles, slightly off center.

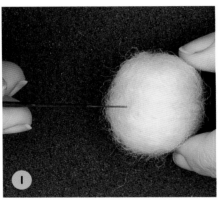

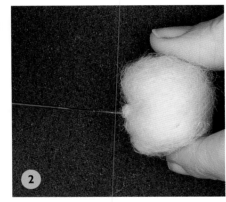

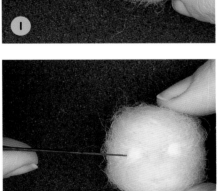

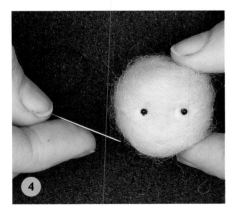

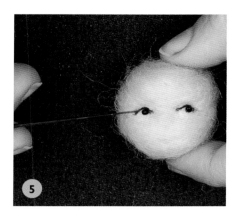

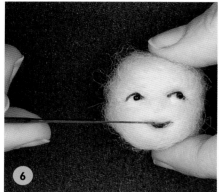

5. Needle a wisp of black wool along the top of the eyes for an eye line.

6. Needle a wisp of black wool underneath the doll's nose for a mouth.

7. Needle a wisp of orange wool underneath the black wool to make lips.

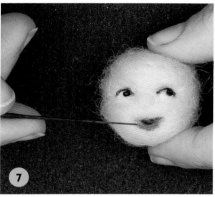

DOLL BODY/KIMONO

8. Measure a 2" × 12" (5.1 × 30.5 cm) piece of orange wool and roll it into a 2½" (6.4 cm) long barrel shape. Needle the surface to help hold the shape.

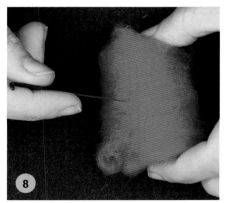

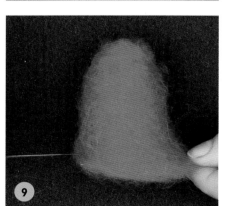

9. To make the kimono shape, gently pull some loose wool at one end of the dress and needle so that it looks like it has a train.

10. Wrap a piece of gold wool around the middle of the kimono and needle to hold it in place.

(continued)

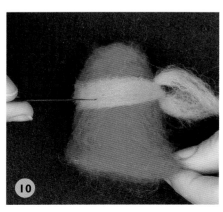

11. Tie the gold wool in a knot on the back of the kimono.

12. To make sleeves, fold two 2" (5.1 cm) long pieces of orange wool in half. Needle the sleeves flat and leave the fibers loose at one end to help attach the sleeves to the kimono.

13. Position the loose fibers of the sleeves on the top-side of the kimono and needle to attach.

14. Roll two wisps of flesh-colored wool into balls and needle them at the end of the sleeves for hands.

15. Position the doll's head on top of the body and needle to attach.

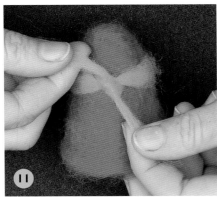

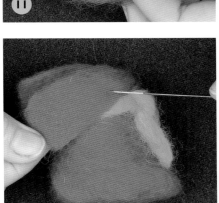

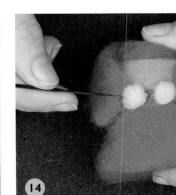

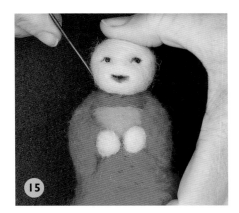

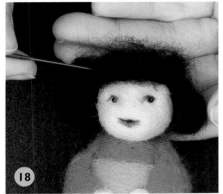

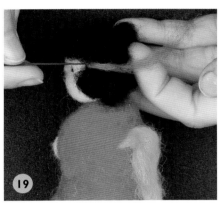

HAIR

16. Lay a 3" (7.6 cm) piece of black wool on top of the doll's head and needle down the middle part to attach the wool to the head. Add more wool and needle until the doll's head is covered with the black wool.

17. Roll two wisps of black wool into bun shapes and needle them on the sides of the doll's head.

18. Needle a wisp of black wool along the doll's forehead to make bangs.

19. Needle a piece of orange wool on the middle of each bun to add decoration to the doll's hair. You can gently twist a paper cocktail umbrella into the doll's hand for added detail.

inspiration gallery

about the author

Artist, teacher, and author Laurie Sharp has been making things since she was a young child. In the past eight years, needle felting and working with wool have been her greatest passions. As an early childhood educator, Laurie finds much inspiration for her artwork from the children she works with and the stories she shares with them.

Currently, Laurie lives in the Pacific Northwest with her husband and business partner, Kevin Sharp. A professional photographer, Kevin took all of the photos for the book, as well as for their first book together, *Wool Pets*.

resources

Woolpets
Laurie and Kevin Sharp
19566 Augusta Ave. N.E.
Suquamish, WA 98392
360-930-0942
www.woolpets.com
Needle felting kits and supplies

A Child's Dream Come True
1223-D Michigan St.
Sandpoint, ID 83864
www.achildsdream.com
Wool felt fabric and felting
supplies

Joann's Fabrics and Crafts
www.Joann.com
Craft supplies and felt
Stores located nationwide

Michael's Arts and Crafts
www.michaels.com
Craft Supplies and other
materials
Stores located nationwide

Magic Cabin
www.magiccabin.com
Craft supplies and wool felt

Nova Natural Toys
www.novanatural.com
Waldorf-inspired toys, craft
supplies, felting kits, and roving

Weir Dolls and Crafts
www.weirdolls.com
Felting supplies, wool felt, doll-
and toy-making kits.

Birgitte Krag Hansen
www.feltmaking.com
Author, artist, and teacher,
Birgitte has authored several
needle felting books and has
a beautiful website full of
inspirational images.

FeltCrafts
www.feltcrafts.com
Supplies, kits, and needle felting
machines

Blue Goose Glen
www.bluegooseglen.com
Needle felting supplies, kits, and
roving.

patterns

Finger Puppets

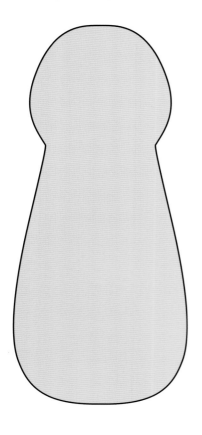

Felt Book House

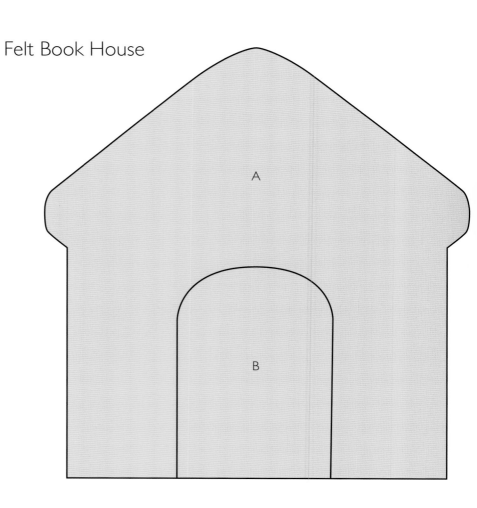

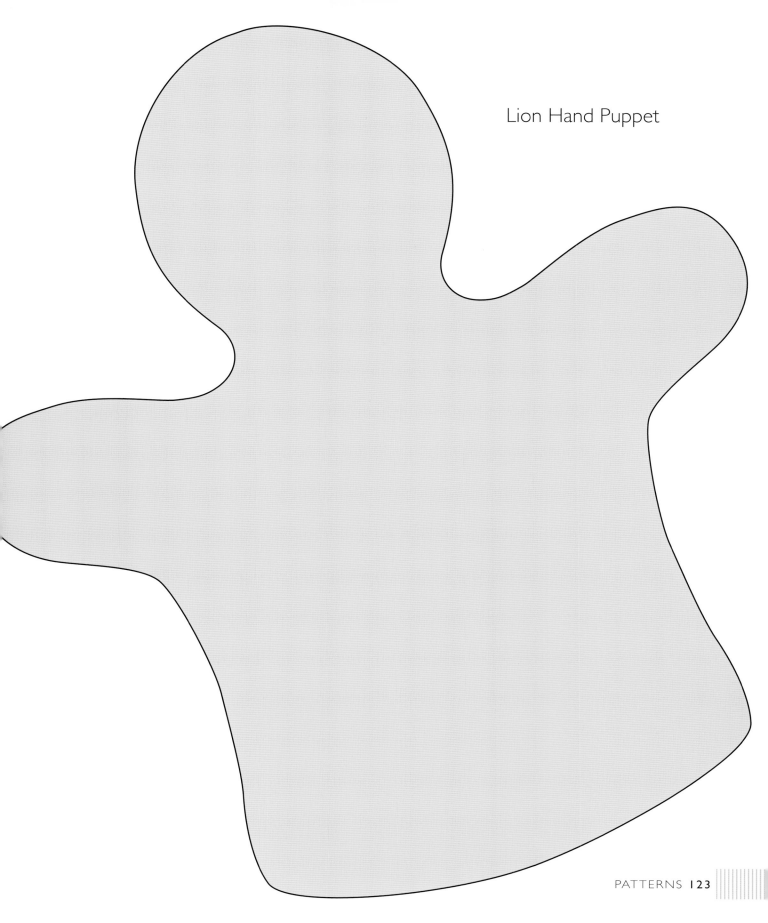

Lion Hand Puppet

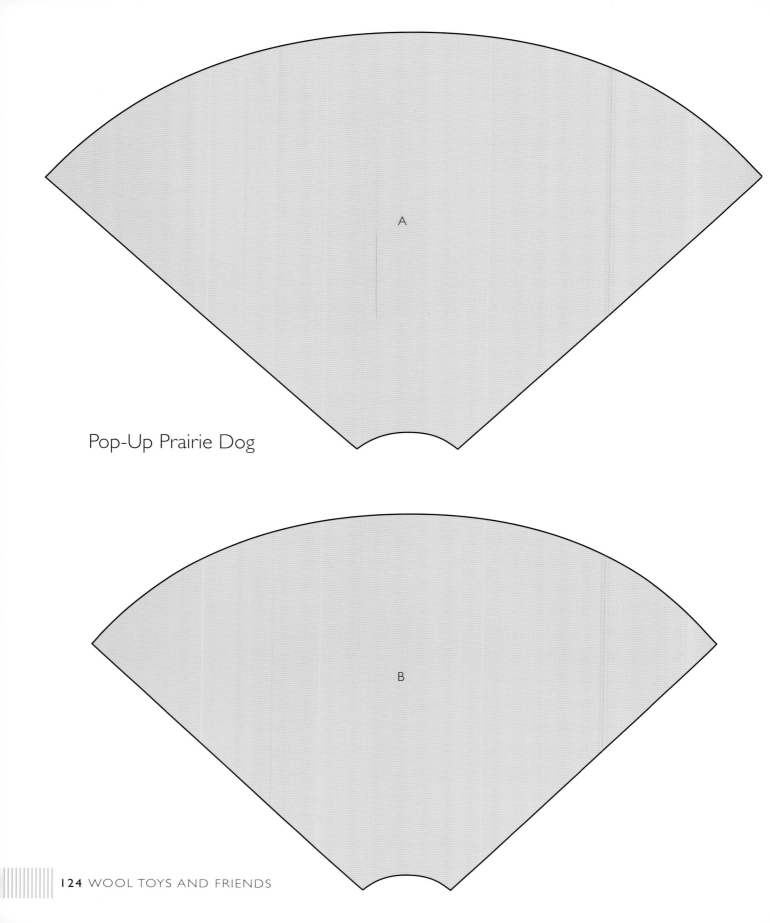

Pop-Up Prairie Dog

A

B

Starfish

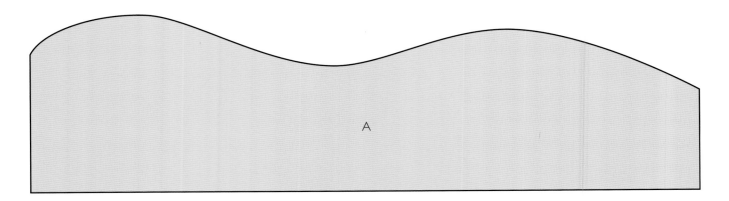

A

Felt Book Waves

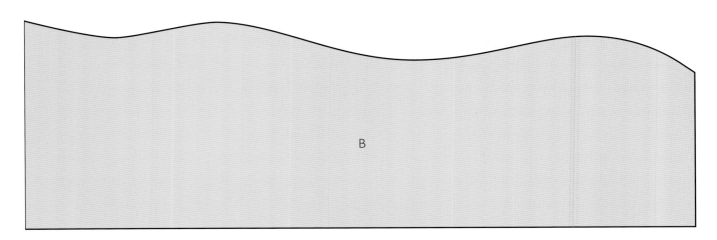

B

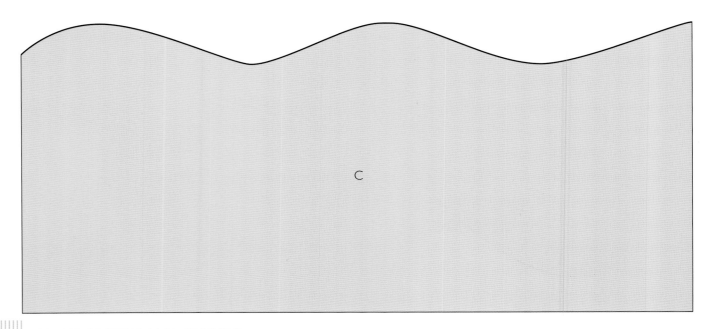

C

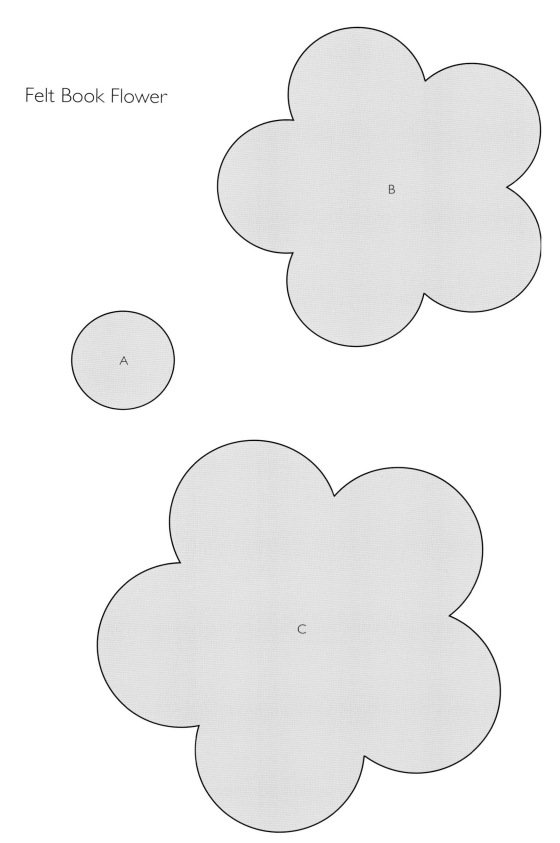

Felt Book Flower

A

B

C

Felt Book Tree

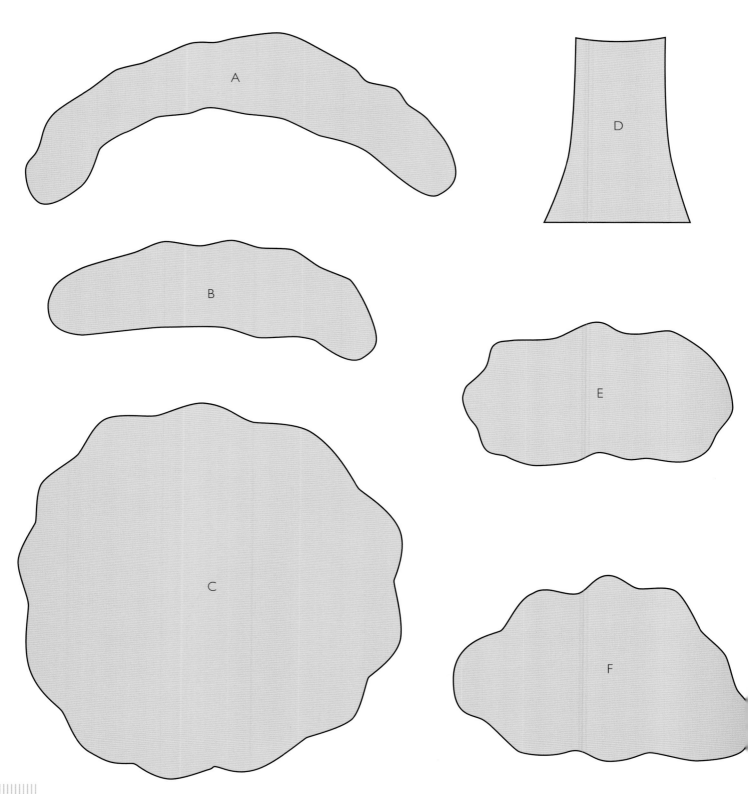

A

D

B

E

C

F